Early Childhood Care and Education

Law, Policy and Practice

Early Childhood Care and Education

Law, Policy and Practice

Dr. Amaresh Chandra Sahoo

Delta Book World
New Delhi-110 002

First Published in 2018
ISBN 978-93-85719-09-7

Published by **Abhishek Goel** on behalf of

Delta Book World
G-4, Prahlad House
4832/24, Ansari Road
New Delhi - 110 002 (India)

Tel.: 011-4707 2321
E-mail: deltabookworld@gmail.com

PRINTED IN INDIA

Dedicated in the memory of
my beloved mother and father

Late Smt. Sulochana Sahoo
&
Late Shri Panchanan Sahoo

Foreword

Knowledge is power - this insight is at least four centuries old, formulated by philosopher Francis Bacon during the Enlightenment. His statement has lost nothing in terms of relevance and significance: Knowledge is power, and education is the fundamental precondition for political development, democracy and social justice. Education empowers the people to develop their potentialities and capacities. It has been proven to have effects on reducing poverty and violence and shown to contribute to individual happiness, feelings of self-worth and resiliency. It gives us knowledge of the world around us and changes it into something better. It develops in us a perspective of looking at life and helps us to build opinions and have points of view on things in life. It develops confidence and helps in building personality of a person.

Education is very important tool for everyone to succeed in life and get something different. It helps a lot in lessening the challenges of life. Knowledge gained throughout the education period enables each and every individual confident about their life. It opens up various doors to the opportunities of achieving better prospects in life. It brings feeling of equality among all people in the society and promotes growth and development of the country. It plays a paramount role in the modern technological world. Many awareness programmes has been run by the government in enhancing the value of education in rural areas. Better education is very necessary for all to go ahead in life and get success. School education plays a great role in everyone's life. The whole education has been divided into three divisions such as the primary education that prepares the base which helps throughout the life, secondary education which prepares the path for further study and higher secondary education prepares the ultimate path of the future and whole life. Thus good or bad education decides that which type of person we are. Education has many benefits and has positive impact in our life. An educated person is an asset for any country. In today's world, human capital is considered as the best national resource. On one hand we can explore better opportunities and on the other hand, the entire nation would be benefited from our works. From time immemorial, India has been conscious of the importance of education for complete development of a society. Ever since the Vedic age, education has been imparted to succeed generations in Gurukuls and this education did not constitute only bookish knowledge of Vedic chants.

True education is that by which the individual is strengthened and can be away from sorrow. There should be no timidity, there should be joy and a sense of mental fulfillment – this is knowledge. Without knowledge, we remain depressed in life. Whoever is depressed, understand that he lacks knowledge. So, ignorance has to be eliminated, and next, injustice has to be put to an end. Lack of education is a key factor of poverty and absence of sufficient income/earnings can't overcome the education poverty. In the Millennium Development Goals (MDGs) and the Poverty Reduction Strategy Paper (PRSP) human capital is considered as a weapon against poverty reduction.

In developing countries the social returns of primary education are much higher. Many countries around the world are beginning to realize the importance of education and are investing in it significantly. Making education available to 100 percent of people around the world is one way to ensure that poverty declines. How education removes darkness of ignorance in life and makes it joyful is reflected in this book "Early Childhood Care and Education: Law, Policy and Practice."

It is an immense pleasure for me to write a foreword for this book of Amaresh Chandra Sahoo. The topic is quite relevant in the sense that it throws light to the Right to Education Act and brought a kind of remarkable transformation of Indian Polity. The writer has analysed the requirement of Early Childhood Care and Education (ECCE) for all round development of the child looking into its importance in the present context. He has attempted to ascertain the situation of ECCE after the incorporation of the new provision relating to the young children under Article 45 of the constitution by 86th amendment Act 2002. Early childhood care and education is a foundation stage which establishes physical cognitive, mental development of a child in order to create a strong coping mechanism for his formal education.

The writer explores the context and examines the subject and enlightens us that ECCE is a globally & rapidly used terminology and is acknowledged everywhere. He had justified that the quality ECCE helps in reducing the dropout rates, wastage and stagnation etc at primary stages and results in higher school attainment.

Looking at the importance of ECCE, the writer has analysed the countries having similar socio political system, geographical regimes, socio cultural affinity, economic growth and other patterns comparatively and also has brought a comparative study about it. The book explores the relevance of ECCE in United States of America, United Kingdom, Australia, China, Brazil, France, Switzerland, Canada, Thailand, Philippines, Spain, Srilanka, Indonesia and Arab countries and reviews the existing policies, programs relating to ECCE in global context with a comparative perspective. The writer also explains about Jean-Jacques Rousseau's philosophy of education. Rousseau who is remembered in the mental horizon of the posterity for his penning of immortal classic "Emile" in 1762 called "attention to the importance of the early childhood years" and changed the history of education. Undoubtedly Amaresh Chandra Sahoo's book is a high quality book explaining the important aspect of early childhood care and education.

Prof. B. N. Ray
Director, (Research)
Kalinga Institute of Social Sciences
Bhubaneswar, Odisha

Acknowledgements

I express my sincere gratitude to Mr. Pramod Kishore Acharya, senior researcher of NLUO. He not only guides me but also inspired a lot for this work. Being a great academician, progressive minded educationalist, he rendered his valuable time and advice me. I acknowledge my sincere thanks to him for his valuable suggestions, inspiring guidance, constant help and encouragement at every stage.

I would like to extend my thankful gratitude to Prof. B.N Ray, former professor of Delhi University and presently the senior researcher of KITT and KISS University who inspired me a lot for the completion of this book. I am also thankful to my in laws Mrs. Arati Mitra and Mr. Dilip Kumar Mitra and my wife Mrs. Mausumi Mitra for their continuous support and encouragement to complete this work in time.

The preparation of this book could have been made possible due to CLAP and the contribution of many people in various ways. A great opportunity will be missed if I do not acknowledge the contribution and support provided by various individuals and institutions.

This book is dedicated in the memory of my beloved mother late Smt. Sulochana Sahoo and father late Sri Panchanan Sahoo.

I wish to acknowledge the immense benefit I have derived from the research publications of various authors, which have enriched my understanding of the subject.

Dr. Amaresh Chandra Sahoo
Department of Political Science
Capital Law College
Bhubaneswar (Odisha)

Preface

Early Childhood Care and Education (ECCE) is a potential condition to accomplish the holistic development of the child. The importance of ECCE completes formulation of child's physical, cognitive and other psycho-social development. It has been recognized through many research based evidence. In this context not many research doctrines are available to provide empirical findings to relate ECCE as an enabling condition for the realization of Right to Education. This book titled, "Early Childhood Care and Education: Law, Policy and Practice" has been brought out where the author has made an attempt to analyses ECCE in a right based perspective in the context of Article 21(A) of the constitution of India and other International practice for the young children.

This book justifies how the quality ECCE helps in reducing the dropout rates, wastage and stagnation etc at primary stages and results in higher school attainment and also helps in the development of children in a variety of ways including group socialization, infusion of healthy habits, and stimulation of creative learning process. This book ascertain the situation of ECCE after the incorporation of the new provision relating to the rights of the young children under Article 45 of the constitution by 86th amendment Act 2002.

This book also justifies the essentiality of ECCE for the inclusion in the Constitution of India from Directive Principles of State Policy to Fundamental Rights category looking into its importance. This book explores the relevance of early childhood care and education in many developing and developed countries of the world.

It also explains about the importance of the concept of Early Childhood Care and Education for its inclusion under the Fundamental Rights category. At the same time the positive impact of ECCE is also described in a variety of ways from different perspectives. It will create a debate and discussion among the intellectuals, Statesman, Policy makers to think about this.

Contents

Abbreviations

ADI - Average Dietary Intake
AIIMS - All India Institute of Medical Science
ASHA - Asha Worker
AWH - Anganwadi Helper
BPL - Below Poverty Line
CDPO - Child Development Project Officer
CECDE - Center for Early Childhood Development and Education
CRC - Convention on the Rights of the Child
CSC - Child Study Center
CTC - Central Technical Committee
D.P.S.P - Directive Principles of State Policy
DECPE - Department of Early Childhood and Primary Education
DFA - Darkar Framework for Action
DSWO - District Social Welfare Officer.
ECCE - Early Childhood Care and Education
ECE - Early Childhood Education
EFA - Education for All
GER - Gross Enrolment Ratio
HDI - Human Development Index
ICDS - Integrated Child Development Service
IIPS - International Institute of Population Science
IMR - Infant Mortality Rate

MCS	- Model Cluster School
MDG	- Millennium Development Goals
MMR	- Maternal Mortality Ratio
NAEYC	- National Association for the Education of Young Children
NCAER	- National Council for Applied Economic Research
NCERT	- National Council of Educational Research and Training
NECCE	- National Early Childhood Care & Education
NEL	- National Education Law
NGO	- Non-Government Organization
NIPCCD	- National Institute of Public Cooperation and Child Development
NNM	- National Nutrition Mission
NPA	- National Plan of Authority
NPE	- National Policy on Education
NPEGEL	- National Programme for the Education of Girl at the Elementary Level
ONPEC	- Office of National Primary Education Commission
OPEPA	- Odisha Primary Education Program Authority
POA	- Program of Action
PSE	- Pre-School Education
RDA	- Recommended Dietary Allowance
RTE	- Right to Education
SAARC	- South Asia Association for Regional Cooperation
SNP	- Special Nutrition Programme
SSA	- Sarva Sikshya Abhiyan
UEE	- Universalisation of Elementary Education
UK	- United Kingdom
UNCRC	- United Nations Convention on the Rights of the Child
UNDP	- United Nations Development Programme
UNESCO	- United Nation's Educational Scientific and Cultural Organization
WCD	- Women and Child Development Department
WSC	- World Summit for Children

1

Early Childhood Care and Education: Legal System

Early Childhood Care and Education (ECCE) is currently an internationally used terminology, is a subject matter of immense importance in the present context for the all round development of the child. As a wide range of the programme Early Childhood Care and Education aims at the physical, moral, cognitive and social development of the child. It is the foundation stone basing on which the life of an individual is built up. Childhood is a state of wonder – a time when the world is fresh and every event is interesting. The terminology, Early Childhood Care and Education (ECCE) in India is an integrated package of measures of ICDS led by Govt. of India designed for all round development of the young children from the age group of 3 to 6 years.

The significance of the early childhood care and education is being increasingly acknowledged every where in the world. The aim of early childhood education is a versatile development of child's personality. Besides education and teaching, early childhood education also includes a basic care. Early childhood education helps a child to be ready and mature for a smooth transition to school environment.[1] As an important aspect of development in every child's period, the early childhood period is embodied with the issues of care and education. All these concepts are integrated in a nomenclature called "Early Childhood Care and Education".

The term 'care' in the nomenclature requires that the health, nutrition, psychological and emotional needs of the children have to be met adequately for their holistic development. Early childhood being a precious period of every individual. Early years of children's lives is cascaded with fastest brain development, and physical growth. Early childhood period is the most critical period when the foundations are laid for the lifelong development and the realization of full potentiality of the children. Young children from this stage are to be provided opportunities and experiences that lead to all round development including physical, mental, social and psychological readiness. An enabling environment for children would be one that is rich, allows children to explore, experiment and freely express themselves and one that is embodied in social relations that give a sense of warmth, security and trust. ECCE supports children's survival, growth, development and his learning including health, nutrition and hygiene and other development from birth to entry in to primary school.

Quality ECCE also helps in reducing the dropout rate, wastage and stagnation etc at primary stages and over long run it results in higher school attainment and higher occupational status. Thus ECCE helps in the development of children in a variety of ways like;

- It improves group socialization
- Infusion of healthy habits
- Stimulation of creative learning process and
- Enhanced scope for all round development of the children.

This is also a critical period having stimulating effect towards development of child's learning, cognitive, language acquisition, and communication skills.

Early childhood is defined 'as a period from birth to six years old; a time of remarkable brain development; and a period that lays the foundation for subsequent[2] learning' (UNESCO; EFA Global Monitoring Report-2007). The term 'education' covers learning, a process of acquiring knowledge, skills, habits, and attitudes in order to prepare the young child to enter the formal education system. (NCERT; National Curriculum Framework-2005 Position Paper; National Focus Group on Early Childhood Care and Education). Early childhood care and education assumes great significance for holistic development of child, which helps children to develop readiness (i.e. in terms of physical and cognitive readiness) for primary schooling. ECCE is central to the lives of every young child. (Edward Melhuish. Konstantinos; ECCE- International Perspectives, 2006; Ruteldge Publication).

Conceptual Analysis of ECCE

The concept Early Childhood Care and Education commonly referred to as ECCE has been used in separate nomenclature in different documents. While ECCE has invariably been used in the documents of UNESCO, ECCD is referred in the document of Organization for Economic Cooperation and Development (OECD), and Early Childhood Development (ECD) is being referred in the documents of UNICEF and World Bank. Although, these have been used in different context, the focus remains the same, i.e.;

(i) Early development of the brain occurs in first two years of life;

(ii) Children learns in the fastest pace during the age of 0-6 years;

(iii) Foundation for a person's learning is laid in the early childhood years;

(iv) Children who receive pre-school education get ready for primary education in the right age and perform better in school, and are less likely to be dropout.[3]

Since the focus of the ECCE is concerned, it would be more pertinent to give precise meaning of the concept. In general sense, ECCE refers to the combination of physical, cognitive, emotional development and social learning of a child. According to Wikipedia Encyclopedia, Early Childhood Education (ECE) is a pedagogical approach for the education of children ranging from birth to six years of age. Early childhood is a vital period of human development where development occurs in different domains, which are interrelated.

According to UNESCO Early Childhood Care and Education programme that attend health, nutrition, learning which have provisions for children's holistic development. The term Early Childhood Care and Education (ECCE) refers to 'a philosophy of providing opportunities and experiences to young children up to age of 8 years in order to promote their holistic development. The span of early childhood is extended to 6 years in order to ensure a gradual and smooth transition of the child from pre-primary to primary education.'[4]

Early Childhood Care and Education refers to "wide range of programmes, all aimed at the physical, cognitive, and social development of children before they enter to primary school theoretically form birth to age 7 and 8. It is a diverse area of learning ranges from pre-primary education, which is integrated with the national education system via kindergartens where care, play and education are all included with more informal and often home based activities."[5]

The Early Childhood Care and Education has dual importance; first it directly influences the child development, and second is potential contribution to programme of universal elementary education."[6] Early childhood care and education not only fosters children's development but also enable them to adopt o the practice and environment of primary school. Thus, ECCE programme should cover child development and school readiness activities with the objective of promoting;

(i) Child health and physical development;

(ii) Social and emotional development;

(iii) Attitude towards learning;

(iv) Language and communication skills; and

(v) Cognitive development and problem solving skills.

Early Childhood Care and Education is an important aspect of educational development of the country. The 21st century has witnessed phenomenal educational developments in India – in terms of law, policy and plans. As early childhood education is seen as preparatory ground for school education, education laws and policies have tended to put increasing focus on early childhood care and education. Early childhood education, pre-school education should be recognized as integral part of the education system.

The adoption of 86th Constitutional Amendment Act, 2002 is a phenomenal in the history of the Constitution of India. Fifty-two years had been taken to shift the provision of free and compulsory education from Directive Principles of state policy to Fundamental Rights. By virtue of this amendment, State is under constitutional obligation to devise a legal framework in order to ensure the mandate of Article-21 (A) for providing free and compulsory education to all children in the aged of 6-14 years. The 86th Amendment has, not only surfaced and sharpened the education debate, but also put the actions and performances of the Union Government as well as State Governments under the public scrutiny. However, the most unceremonious aspect of the 86th constitutional amendment is the division of the provision of Article-45 into two parts.[7] Like;

1. The right of free and compulsory education is recognized as a fundamental right of 6-14 year aged children and;
2. The subject of early childhood care and education for 0-6 year children has found place in Article-45 that is under the Directive Principles of State Policy (DPSP) instead of in the chapter of Fundamental Rights.

The Directive Principles of State Policies are only directives to the State. The line of difference between Part-III & Part-IV of the Constitution (Fundamental Rights & DPSP) rests on the legal status. Unlike, the Fundamental Rights, no one may approach the judiciary for enforcement of any the DPSP. In constitutional terminology, while the fundamental rights are justifiable, directive principles are non justiciable. It is the moral and political discretion of the political party or alliance in power how and when to act upon it.

ECCE is recognized as potential elements that positively contribute towards the learning outcome of the child, averting early childhood care and education from right to education is impertinent, as far 86th amendment is concerned. However, by putting ECCE in Directive Principles, the constitutional direction for the state to formulate policy and legal framework in order to ensure ECCE to all children below the age of six years. The legal policy framework of ECCE has to focus on universal access and enrolment of children in pre-primary education, and for bringing improvement in the quality of ECCE service, improvement in infrastructure, monitoring and supervision of service delivery system, development of pre-school education curriculum, and development of human resources etc.

It is persuasively argued that early childhood care and education (Article-45) and right to free and compulsory education (Article-21 (A) does not stand apart. Virtually, Article-45 is an enabling provision for the successful realization of fundamental right to education.[8] This is blatantly viewed that right to education may be rightly realized if ECCE is prioritized in education development agenda and early childhood care and education is recognized as a right.

Numbers of years have been passed since the adoption of 86th amendment act. During this period, a substantial progress might have been made in terms of developing policies and programmes in order to have effective governance of ECCE service. Here a comprehensive analysis of the policies and schemes for delivering the institutional service for ECCE is made. An attempt has to be made generosity of approach for securing a legal framework for ECCE as the statutory back up to Article-45 of the Constitution of India. The importance of having a law on early childhood care and education is based on the assumption that it would result in adequate provisioning of institutional service for improving accessibility of children to pre-school education and policy focus for quality up- gradation. Above all, the legislation is seen as an enabling framework for improving the quality of ECCE service and ensuring governance accountability.

Background of ECCE

Education has been recognized as the center piece of human development. The International Human Rights Instruments have recognized education as a basic human right. The Right to Education is enshrined as the most affirmed economic, social, and cultural rights in the Universal Declaration of Human Rights. It says, "every one has the right to education, and therefore, education should be free and compulsory at least in the elementary stages and higher forms of education should be accessible to all on merit; education should be directed to the full development of human personality and strengthening of respect for human rights and fundamental freedoms; and parents have a right to choose kind of education given to their children".[9]

The International Covenant on Economic, Social, and Cultural Rights (ICESCR), 1966 also recognized right of everyone to education. The UN Convention on the Rights of the Child (UNCRC), 1989 under Article-28 categorically states that "State Parties recognize the right of the child to education and with a view to achieving this right progressively, they shall in particular make primary education compulsory and available free to all."

The global quest for universal primary education gained momentum from the year 1990 following the World Conference on Education for All (EFA) held in Jomtien, Thailand. At the same time the Darkar Framework for Action-2000 (DFA) adopted in the World Education Forum is seen an extension of the affirmation and commitment made in the World Conference in 1990 for accelerating progress towards education for all.

The Darkar Framework for Action-2000 (DFA)

The DFA is an international framework that devises for inclusive and equitable opportunity of education for all children extending from early childhood care and education to universal elementary education. Recognizing Early Childhood Care and Education (ECCE) as a stimulation that strengthens cognitive development and helps in preparing children for primary education, DFA pledges for expanding and improving comprehensive early childhood care and education, especially for most vulnerable and disadvantaged children.

With the adoption of DFA, the subject of Early Childhood Care and Education (ECCE) has become an important catalyst for achieving the goal of Universal Elementary Education (UEE).[10] India as a signatory state to the EFA (Education for All) and is committed to achieve DFA goal by 2015 in terms of providing good quality Early Childhood Care and Education and Primary Education. India is a signatory to these key international instruments that guarantees right to education and country has been under commitment to translate the internationally acclaimed doctrine in the domestic spheres. In 2002, after sixty-two years of the enforcement of the Constitution, India provides constitutional guarantee for Free and Compulsory Education to 6-14 year children as a matter to secure right to education

Demands for Right to Education

India had a long history of organized education. However, the concept of state education system had evolved in India during the British Rule when East India Company accepted the responsibility for education through Charter Act, 1813. Since then demand for right to education was stimulated in the country.

Demand during Freedom Movement

The demand for right to education was made during the freedom struggle. This is evidenced from the demand of state-sponsored free education for all children for minimum of 4 years by Dadabhai Naroji and Jyothiba Phule before the British Government appointed Education Commission in 1882, commonly known as Hunter Commission. This demand was indirectly acknowledged in commission report as the Commission made a recommendation for mass education in India. On 18th March, 1910, Gopal Krishna Gokhale moved a resolution in Imperial Legislative Council for seeking of Free and Compulsory Primary Education in India. The public demand for compulsory primary education was sharpened in early quarters of the 20th century and between 1918 and 1931 compulsory education laws were passed for most parts of the country by the newly elected State Legislatures in which Indians were in majority. In 1937, Mahatma Gandhi put forward his scheme of *Basic Education* under which education of seven or eight years duration was to be provided for all children. At that time a national consensus was built up with an idea of providing equality of opportunity for education and duty of the State to provide free and compulsory education to all children till they reached the age of 14 years.

The Education Commission led by Sir John Sargent, the then Educational Advisor to the Government of India endorsed the same proposal in the commission report. They were accepted by the British administration and accordingly the educational development plan, popularly known as Sargent Plan, was devised in India in 1944, which put forward proposals to provide free and compulsory basic education to all children in the age group 6-14 over a period of 40 years (1944-1984). There was a national resentment on the Sargent Plan proposal of stretching the period to 40 years. A Committee under the chairmanship of B.G. Kher also proposed that goal of providing free and compulsory education could and should be achieved in a period of 16 years (1944-1960).

Demand in the Constituent Assembly

In spite of consistent demand for right to free and compulsory education during the freedom struggle, there was a debate in the Constituent Assembly on the issue of placing right to education in the category of justiciable or non-justciable right chapter of the Constitution. The Sub-Committee on Fundamental Right of Constituent Assembly had made deliberation to include the right to primary education as justiciable right. However, B. Shiva Rao (pp. 124-126 of the Minutes of the Proceedings of Fundamental Rights Sub-Committee Meeting of March 27, 1947) and Sir Alladi Krishnaswami Ayyar, differing from the majority, were not in favour of its inclusion as justiciable right and same was also the view of K.M. Panikkar.[11]

In the Advisory Committee Meeting, on the suggestion of Pandit Gobind Ballav Pant, it was decided to include the right to primary education as non-justifiable right. The draft Article-45 was very much in the same language as it was incorporated in constitution with significant differences that draft constitution covered the phrase "every citizen is entitled to free primary education". Subsequently, an amendment was moved in the Constituent Assembly to drop the phrase 'primary education'.[12]

Deliberated on the proposal of the Sub-Committee to place Free and Compulsory Education on the list of Fundamental Rights, the Drafting Committee did not agree to that and the same was listed in the Directive Principles of State Policy under Article-45 which stated, "The State shall endeavor to provide, within a period of 10 years from the commencement of this Constitution, for free and compulsory education for all children until they complete the age of fourteen years". Putting education in the non-justifiable chapter, the framers did not abridge the significance of education as human right.

The Constitution, from the beginning, has considered education a basic right and directed the State to provide equality of educational opportunity to all. The constitutional wisdom was very much reflected in Article-41 of the Directive Principle that eloquently expressed "The State, shall within the limits of its economic capacity and development, make effective provision for securing the Right to Education". The underlying provision of Article-45 was seen as the constitutional desire to achieve the goal within a stipulated timeframe in order to have an effective realization of right to education.

Demand in Education Commissions

Since the enforcement of the Constitution i.e. January 26, 1950, Government of India has made numbers of efforts in a bid to bring improvements in educational planning, development and systems. In course of the development, a good number of policies have been developed on the recommendation of the Education Commission. The First Indian Education Commission (Kothari Commission)1964-68 made recommendation, among several recommendations, of a common school system with a view to eliminating inequality in educational opportunities.

The Commission's recommendation was duly acknowledged in National Policy on Education-1968 that viewed for equalization of educational opportunity and sought to adopt common school system in order to promote social cohesion.[13] Furtherance to it the National Policy on Education-1986 promised to achieve the goal of universal elementary education and to take measures to achieve a common school system.[14] However, both the policies did not go the extent to explore the legal status of free and compulsory education, as stated in Article-45. Even the NPE-1968 retained the status of education in the Directive Principles.[15] However, the recommendation of Acharya Ramamurti Committee-1990 was the first official recommendation for inclusion of right to education in fundamental rights chapter.[16]

Demand in Judicial Pronouncement

The right to education demand has been kept alive by the civil society in the context of verdict of the Supreme Court that showed keen interest of the judiciary in making education as a fundamental right. On many occasions, the Supreme Court has come forward to decide the legal context of the directive principles. The Supreme Court of India delivered a historic judgment in 1992 in the case of Mohini Jain vs. State of Karnataka[17] where the judiciary hold the view that 'the right to education" springs from Right to Life and is a concomitant to Fundamental Rights enshrined under Part-III of the Constitution and that "every citizen has a right to education under the Constitution'. Subsequently, the Supreme Court had to reexamine the above-mentioned in the case of Unnikrishnan vs. State of Andhra Pradesh[18].

The Court pronounced that 'though right to education is not stated expressively as a fundamental right, it is implicit in and flows from the right to life guaranteed under Article-21 and must be construed in the light of the Directive Principles of the Constitution. The 'Right to Education' understood in the context of Article-45 and 41 means;

(a) every child of this country has a right to free education until he completes the age of fourteen years; and

(b) after a child completes fourteen years, his right to education is circumscribed by the limits of the economic capacity of the State and its development.

Consequent upon the Apex Court Judgment and Civil Society pressures, Government was forced to initiate an amendment (Eight-third Amendment Bill) in 1997 in order to make education a fundamental right.

The 83rd Amendment proposed to insert Article-21 (A) (State shall provide free and compulsory education to all citizens of the age of six to fourteen years), and to delete the erstwhile Article-45 from the Constitution, as well as to introduce Article-51-A (k) (fundamental duty of parents to provide opportunities for education). In November 2001, the 83rd bill was renumbered as 93rd Amendment Bill, 2001. The 93rd Amendment Bill proposed that former article 45 be amended to provide for early childhood care and education instead of being deleted altogether. Rajya Sabha passed it on 22nd November 2002 and in Lok Sabha on 27th November 2002. The Bill became the Constitution (Eight Sixth Amendment) Act 2002, after assented to by the President of India.

Presently, under Article 21-A of the Constitution, every child between the ages of six and fourteen years has a fundamental right to 'free and compulsory education', which the State shall provide 'in such manner as the State may, by law, determine'. Article-45 of the Directive Principles of the Constitution requires State to provide 'early childhood care and education' for all children until the completion of six years of age. Added to these, Article 51-A (k) imposes a fundamental duty on parents to provide educational opportunities to their children in the age group of six to fourteen years.

Directive Principles: An Instrument of Instructions

The Directive Principles of State Policy (DPSP) in Indian Constitution were the prototype expression of DPSP (Article-45) of the Constitution of Ireland of 1937, which contains "the principles of social policy set forth in Article are intended for general guidance of the *Oireachtas* (Irish Parliament). The application of these principles in making laws shall be the care of the *Oireachtas* by the Court under any of the provisions of the Constitution". The Directive Principles, as embodied in Part-IV of the Constitution are only moral precepts, and general guidance to government. These principles should be made the basis of all executive and legislative action that they may be taking hereafter in the governance of the country".[19] Regarding the DPSP, Granville Austin writes, these along with the Fundamental Rights are 'core of the commitments to the social revolution and the conscience of the Constitution'.[20] Directive Principles of State Policy is the Book of Interpretation.[21]

After thoughtful deliberation in consideration to country's economic capacity, the framers placed the right to education under the Directive Principles of State Policy instead of Fundamental Rights Chapter of the Constitution of India. The Constitution came into force on 26th day of January 1950 and Article-45 expressed that "The State shall endeavour to provide, within a period of ten years of the commencement of this Constitution, for free and compulsory education for all children until they complete the age of fourteen years", Article-41, " State shall, within economic capacity and development, make effective provision for securing right to education" and Article-46, "State shall promote with special care the educational interest of the Schedule Castes and Schedule Tribes".

By setting a proximate goal in Article-45, the founding fathers of the Constitution would not like to see the continuance of illiteracy for a longer period. In addition to the expression of education in Article-45 and other provision of the Directive Principles, there are important dimensions of the constitution that enrich and expand the constitutional vision for education. First, is the expression of *"Equality of Opportunity and to Promote among them all"* in the Preamble of the Constitution deserves special mention as the content of Article-45 had emerged from the edifice of the Preamble. Secondly, access and opportunity to education should be made in consonance with Article-14[22] (equality before law and equal protection of law), Article-15[23] (Right against non-discrimination), and Article-24[24] (Right against exploitation) of Part-III of the Constitution.

Education is Subject of Whom

The Constitution of India, based on the principle of federalism, distributes legislative powers between Parliament and State Legislatures on the basis of three lists - Union List, State List, and Concurrent List – of the Seventh Schedule of the Constitution. The Parliament of India is vested with the residual powers and power to amend the Constitution. Parliament has exclusive power to make laws to any of the matters enumerated in List-I (Union List) and State Legislatures have power to make for List-II (State List). Both Parliament and State Legislatures have power to make law in any matters enumerated in List-III (Concurrent List).

Originally, "Education"[25] was enlisted in the State List. Thus education was the subject matter of State Governments. However, by virtue of 42nd Constitutional Amendment Act of 1976, the subject "Education"[26] was shifted to the Concurrent List. The significance of shifting of education to Concurrent List was justified in the NPE-1986 & 1992, in the words that, union government would accept a large responsibility to reinforce the national and integrative character of education to maintain quality and standard, to study and monitor the educational requirements of the country as a whole in regard to human power for development, to cater the needs of the research and advance study, to look after the international aspects of education, culture, human resource development, and in general, to provide excellence at all levels of the education pyramid through the country." Education in the State is the joint responsibility of the Central Government and State Governments.

The responsibility of education development rests largely with the State Governments. The Government of India, under its constitutional obligation, has the responsibility of making educational policy and national framework to supplement the efforts of the State Governments. The Government of India has taken some policy initiatives in the form of National Policy for Education (NPE)-1986, District Primary Education Programme (DPEP), Sarva Siksha Abhiyan (SSA) and more recently the Right of Children to Free and Compulsory Education Act, 2009. Notably, each education policy is condensed with a target to achieve. The NPE-1986 had a target to achieve complete five years schooling for all children of 11 years of age by the year 1990 and free and compulsory education to all children below 14 years age by 1995. The NPE-1992 (POA) revised the target year to 2000. The DPEP was launched as a major initiative to revitalize the primary education system and to achieve the objective of universalisation of primary education by the year 2000. The SSA, 2000 was a time bound initiatives with the objective to provide elementary education to all children in the age group of 6-14 years by 2010. The objective was set to be achieved in three- phased ways, i.e.;

(i) Children to complete five years of primary schooling by 2007;

(ii) All children to complete eight years schooling by 2010; and

(iii) Universal retention by 2010.

Integrating Pre-Primary Education in School Education

Indian education system comprises of different stages: primary, secondary, higher secondary, graduation, and post-graduation. There are also opportunities for students to go for technical education after completion of secondary or higher secondary education. Even students can prefer professional courses such as management, law, etc. There are three stages of school education in India. It broadly consists of –

(i) Primary education (Class I-V),

(ii) Elementary education (Class VI-VIII) and

(iii) Secondary education (Class IX-X)

With other names in different states of India, school management in India is also not uniform. As education is concurrent subject, as per seventh schedule of the constitution of India, it draws the responsibility of both the government of India and state governments. There are also schools run by missionaries, trust, private bodies, public sectors, and corporations. Majority of children in India are reading in state government's school that is managed by the State Board of Education/State Secondary Board of Education. There are also Central Board of Secondary Education and Council for Indian School Certificate Examination for central government schools. These are also the examining bodies for public and other English medium schools. Opportunities are also provided to children to go for correspondence education through National Open Schools. There are also few international schools in India with western pattern of education and school curriculum. Pre-primary education such as kindergarten in the form LKG and UKG is the integral part of education in public schools and English medium schools and child before entering into the Standard-I shall have to complete minimum 2 years of pre-school education. Pre-primary education is not compulsory for admission in state-run primary schools.

Constitutional Directive and Progress towards Achieving the Goal

The Constitution, under Article-45, directed the State to provide free and compulsory education at the earliest of 1960. In order to obey the constitutional directive, the government made all efforts to achieve the target at the earliest of 1960, precisely by January 26, 1960. Realizing the slow progress, target year has been time and again deferred successively to 1970, 1980, and 1990 and then to 2000. From 1990 onwards, education development planning of the country is seen outcome of India's commitment and affirmation to international declaration/convention.

In March 1990, India signed the World Declaration on Education for All, and Framework for Action to meet Basic Learning Needs adopted at the World Conference on Education for All held in Jometin, Thailand. A decade later in April, 2000, India signed the Darkar Framework of Action and is committed to achieve education for all by 2015.[27] India ratified the UN Convention on the Rights of the Child (CRC-1989) on December 11, 1992 and thereby is obliged to implement the provisions of the Convention, review the progress of its implementation in periodic intervals and report to the UN Committee. The DPEP and SSA policy was the concomitant effect of the global education trend and these have been designed in conjunction with the objectives of DFA.

Despite all the strategic planning, the national goals of universal elementary education and removal of illiteracy have still remained elusive. The fact is substantiated through the statistical information that shows the gruesome and fallible indications of educational achievement in India. Let us elaborate the findings of the national report in order to surmise the educational achievement in India. The flow of educational achievement and development is usually measured through commonly used standards that include literacy rate, and enrolment ratio, dropout rate in different levels of education.

As per Census-2011, the literacy rate in India is 69.8 percent with large inter-state variations. At one end, the proportion of literacy rate is highest in Kerala, that is 90.8 percent, and at the other it is 46.9 percent in Bihar. Aside, regional variation, educational disparities is more pronounced in terms of rural-urban and male-female literacy rates. The literacy rate in rural areas is 59 percent and the corresponding figure in urban areas is 80 percent. Similarly, the male literacy rate is 75.6 percent in comparison to female literacy rate of 53.6 percent. The literacy rate for Schedule Castes and Schedule Tribes population has been much lower than the rest of the population.

The enrolment ratio has two dimensions – Gross Enrolment Ratio (GER), and Net Enrolment Ratio (NER). GER is defined as the percentage of enrolment in primary education (Classes I-V), and Upper Primary Education (Classes V-VIII) or Elementary Education (Classes I-VIII) to the estimated child population in the age group of 6 to below 11 years, 11 to below 14 years or 6-14 years respectively. GER percentage might be more than 100% as it includes the enrolment of under-age and over-age children. NER refers to proportion of child population, of a particular age group (i.e. 6-11, 11-14 or 6-14 year aged group), enrolled in a specific level of schooling, to the total population in that age group.

As per the report[28] of the Ministry of Human Resource Development, Govt. of India, the GER in Primary Classes had gone up from 42.6 percent in 1950-51 to 95.7 percent in 2000-01 and in Upper Primary level, this had progressed to 58.8 percent in 2000-01 from 12.7 percent in 1950-51. The SES of 2005-06 shows that the GER is 111.24 in Primary Classes, 73.63 in Upper Primary Classes, and 96.92 in Elementary Stages (Classes I-VIII). The Seventh All India Educational Survey, 2000 Report upholds that the NER for children in the age group of 6-14 years is 57.5 percent. In simplest sense, of the children in the age group of 6-14 years, 57.5 percent children was enrolled in Classes I- VIII. To decipher further, the NER among 6-11 year aged children in primary classes (Classes I-V) was 62.2 percent and among 11-14 year aged children in Classes VI-VIII, it was 44.8 percent.[29]

The dropout rate is a major indicator to assess the level of success in educational attainment. The disquieting fact is that the dropout rate still remains at the higher side, which means a reasonable proportion of children are dropped from primary and upper primary level. The SES-2006-07 indicates that the rate of drop out in primary classes (Classes I-V) at All-India Level is 25.5 percent with considerable regional disparity. The magnitude of drop out is between 40 to 50 percent in Orissa, Meghalaya, Bihar, Assam and more than 50 percent in Rajasthan, Jharkhand. Dropout rate in Classes I-VIII is 46.03 percent at the all India level. That means only 54 children out of 100 children enrolled in Class-I would complete the elementary education. The dropout rate in elementary level (Classes I-VIII) has been quite high in the State of Andhra Pradesh, Arunachal Pradesh, Meghalaya, Mizoram, Orissa, Rajasthan, Sikkim, Tripura, West Bengal (50-70%), and in Assam, Arunachal Pradesh (70% above). The proportion of drop out is quite higher among the Schedule Castes and Schedule Tribe children. Among SC children, the dropout rate is 35.9 in Primary Level and 53.0 percent in Elementary Level. Among the ST children, the enormity of dropouts is 33.1 and 62.5 in primary and elementary level respectively.

Achieving the Goal of Universal Elementary Education

The SSA was a time-bound initiative of the central government and a flagship programme for universal elementary education. SSA articulated few specific goals in order to realize the objective of Article-21 (A) of the constitution, i.e. right to free and compulsory education of 6-14 year aged children. Here, it is pertinent to have introspection on the progress towards achievement of SSA Goals.

All 6-14 Year Aged Children in Schools

The annual growth rate[30] of enrolment in primary and upper primary level was 4.4% in 2002-03, 5.8% in 2004-05, and 6.3% 2005-06. The net enrolment ratio in primary classes was 73.9% in 2003-04, which had increased to 81.9% in 2004-05.

All Children to Complete Five Years Primary Schooling by 2007

The dropout rate in primary level (Classes 1-V) was 25.43% among all categories of children, 35.96% among the Schedule Caste children, and 33.15% among the Schedule Tribe children for the year 2006-07. Bridging of Gender and Social Category Gaps at Primary Stage by 2007 and at the Elementary Level by 2010. Gender disparity[31] at the primary stage was reduced to 4.2 in 2005-06 from 5.5 in 2002-03. At the upper primary stage the gender disparity[32] remains at the higher side, although the disparity was reduced to 8.8 in 2005-06 from 2002-03.

Universal Retention

The retention rate[33] in primary level was 70.26 and 53.9 in elementary level for 2006-07. The retention rates among SC & ST students are lower than the overall retention rate. Dropout rates among all categories, schedule caste, schedule tribe children in elementary level (Classes I-VIII) in States & Union Territories of India.[34]

Scale of Dropout	All Categories	Schedule Castes	Schedule Tribes
Above 80%			Bihar, Orissa
70-80 %	Assam, Bihar	Assam, Bihar, Orissa	Andhra Pradesh, Assam, Uttar Pradesh, West Bengal
60-70 %	Mizoram, Meghalaya, Orissa, Rajasthan, Sikkim, West Bengal	Andhra Pradesh, Meghalaya, Rajasthan, Sikkim, West Bengal	Tripura, Mizoram, Meghalaya, Gujarat, Madhya Pradesh, Manipur

contd...

50-60%	Andhra Pradesh, Arunachal Pradesh, Tripura	Uttar Pradesh	Arunachal Pradesh, Rajasthan
40-50 %	Gujarat, Jammu & Kashmir, Madhya Pradesh, Manipur, Nagaland, Uttar Pradesh, Dadra & Nagar Haveli	Gujarat, Karnataka, Madhya Pradesh, Punjab, Tripura, Chandigarh	Dadra & Nagar Haveli, Maharashtra, Tamil Nadu,
30-40 %	Karnataka, Nagaland, Chandigarh	Arunachal Pradesh, Delhi	Jammu & Kashmir, Karnataka, Nagaland, Sikkim, Dadra & Nagar Haveli
Below 30 %	Goa, Himachal Pradesh, Kerala, Maharashtra, Punjab, Andaman & Nicobar Island, Daman & Diu, Delhi	Goa, Haryana, Himachal Pradesh, Jammu & Kashmir, Kerala, Maharashtra, Tamil Nadu, Dadra & Nagar Haveli	Kerala, Andaman & Nicobar Island

The enormity of dropout rate even more than five decades of planning and educational development might have been indication wastage of primary education as well lack of efforts in addressing the causes of the dropouts. Recognizing the findings of a survey of the National Sample Survey Organization (NSSO), the National Human Development Report-2001[35], reaffirms that "Children from the poorer sections of the society drop out in the early stages of education, while those from the better off the sections of the society drop out at the later stages. Among the reasons for dropping out from schools one-third of the dropouts were because either the children or their parents were not interested for education. About 26 percent cited school and teaching curricula related factors such as unfriendly atmosphere in schools, doubts about the usefulness of schooling and inability to cope with studies as reasons for their dropping out."[36] Another government report[37] substantiates that one-fourth of the girl children and two-fifth of the male children has dropped out of school due their disinterest in studies.

The child's interest in education and adoptation in school environment would have seen paramount elements for the success of UEE. In order to have acceleration of primary education, the children of pre-primary school aged should have opportunity to receive good quality early childhood care and education. It is well proved that improved access to early childhood care and education can enhance education outcomes and reduce the drop out rates. Early childhood care and education strengthens cognitive development and helps in preparing the children for school. Unfortunately, in India no effective planning has been made to provide ECCE service to all children. Among the children entered in primary education, nearly three-fourths of them have not received pre-school education.

Conclusion

Many of the research findings have proved that ECCE has the potential to make a big difference in terms of access to primary schools, progression through schools and learning outcomes. The factual research evidence was the guiding principles for formulating the Darkar Framework of Action of EFA-2000 that devises for expanding and improving early childhood care and education. The 86th amendment to the constitution was the outcome of India's commitment to DFA. While revising Article-45, the amendment has put right of 6-14 year aged children to free and compulsory education in the chapter of Fundamental Rights and early childhood care and education of under 6-year aged children in the framework of constitution. ECCE under Article-45 of the constitution is a directive to government to devise administrative and legislative framework for delivering the early childhood care and education service to the children. The constitution in the present framework has seen both Articles 45 and 21 (A) are complementary and inseparable. In conformity with the constitutional directives, government is required to formulate legal policy framework to regulate the ECCE service.

In order to fulfill the constitutional obligation, ECCE service should have been one of important priorities of the government of India. In addition to the programmes already under implementation, new dimensions of service delivery should have been explored to universalize ECCE to all with quality.

However, no substantial efforts have so far been made to ensure ECCE. Still Integrated Child Development Service (ICDS) is seen as the major programme for children and through it early childhood care and education service is being delivered in the form of non-formal pre-school education.The Integrated Child Development Services Programme was started in 1975 to tackle the malnutrition among children, mothers and adolescent women, and to provide pre-school education to children below the age of six years as well as basic health care. Conceptually, ICDS is a vital programme for the welfare of the children and it delivers services through a network of ICDS centers, commonly known as Anganwadi Centers.

The situational analysis of the state of early childhood care and education in India with reference to constitutional provision of Article-45, policies and schemes relating to young children, programmatic interventions, and 11th Five-Year Plan approach indicates that early childhood care and education is not recognized as a right of children. While early childhood care and education is a privilege for the children of affluent and elite parents, many children of poor, marginalized and disadvantaged communities are being deprived of getting opportunity to receive ECCE. The very important of ECCE is pre-primary education, which enables the child to develop readiness for primary education. Following the incorporation of ECCE in Article-45 of Directive Principles of Indian Constitution, government has recognized early childhood care and education as a core issue for holistic development of the child.[38]

In order to translate the constitutional principles in practice, government of India has integrated early childhood care and education in the form of non-formal pre-school education in the Integrated Child Development Services (ICDS) scheme. Even though ICDS programme is conceptually holistic, comprehensive and integrated, the pre-school education service is either poorly implemented or almost neglected. This is quite evident in NFHS-III survey report. It shows that only 32.9 percent of children utilized any service from the Anganwadis. 26.3 percent children received food supplements and went to AWCS for pre-school education. ICDS today reaches out to 23 million children through its pre-school programmes. The national evaluation of ICDS showed that children who got the experience of ICDS programme had better nutritional status, better immunization coverage, and were in large number in schools and continued to do so. The evaluation also showed that 50-60 percent of ICDS children were able to count numbers 1-50 while smaller percentage could recognize and name objects (National Institute of Public Cooperation and Child Development, 1997). However there are many other studies, which show that pre-school component of the ICDS programmes, is very weak. The PSE component of the ICDS programme fails to make any significant impact on children due to lack of learning materials.

The problem lies with the policy approach as early childhood care and education is not integrated with the education. ICDS programme does not have the balance linkage between health, nutrition and pre-primary education. ICDS is a programme of basic health (i.e. immunization, health check-up) and supplementary feeding rather than a programme for early childhood education (i.e. pre-primary education). From policy approach to actual implementation, there are plenty of problems ICDS particularly related to pre-school activities. Pre-school education at Anganwadi centers is hampered largely due to:

(i) Lack of basic infrastructure (i.e. building, space, playground & game materials, learning kits),

(ii) Untrained or inadequately trained pre-school instructor (AWW),

(iii) Absence of standard pre-school curriculum indicating learning methods for preschool activities, language to be used for communication;

(iv) Lack of monitoring and supervision;

(v) Aabsence of community participation.

References

1. Early Years children promote Health, The Child to Child Trust.
2. Child Psychology- Ramnath Sharma and Rachana Sharma.
3. Arunima Guide lines, ICDS, WCD, and Govt. of India.
4. Child Care & Education, Tina Bruce and Carolyn Meggitt.
5. Annual Repor, Ministry of Tribal Affairs; Government of India.
6. Census of India (2011).
7. UNESCO: Education for All Global Monitoring Report (2007).
8. United Nations Convention on the Rights of the Child.
9. UNICEF: Progress for Children; A World Fit for Children Statistical Review (Number 6, December 2007).

10. Exploring the Rights of the Child in Early Childhood, A CLAP Publication.
11. Early Childhood matters, Bernad Van Leer Foundation, Neitherland.
12. RTE Act, 2009 and State Rules.
13. National Coordination Forum Education for All 2003
14. HAQ: Centre for Child Rights: Status of Children in India Inc.2005.
15. Working Group on Children Under Six: Strategies for Children Under Six Published in Economic & Political Weekly, December 29, 2007.
16. Walter Barker: Early Childhood Care & Education: The Challenge; Bernard van Leer Foundation.
17. Early childhood Matters' Critical thinkings, BernadVan leer foundation.
18. Early Years children- Promote health, case studies on child to child and Ealy care and Development-The child to child trust childhood care and Education.
19. Ensuring children their childhood, V.V Giri National Labour Institute, New Delhi.
20. Education watch oriss, Citizens report on quality elementary education-2006.
21. Education for all by 2015, will we make it, UNICEF Report.
22. National Health Policy (2002)
23. National Nutrition Policy (1993)
24. National Rural Health Mission (2005)
25. National Plan of Action for Children (2005)
26. National Charter for Children (2004)
27. Commission for Protection of Child Rights Act (2005)
28. Integrated Child Protection Scheme (ICDS)
29. A case study on children, Dr. Bikash Das, A CLAP Publication, 2006
30. A text book on child psychology, Dr. Ramnath Sharma, A Rajhons publication, Meerut University.

31. Early childhood care and Education, principles and practices by J.C. Agrawala and C.Gupta, Shipra publication.
32. Play activities for child development: A guide to pre-School education teacher, Mina Swaminathan, Prem Daniel.
33. History and philosophy of pre-Primary and Nursery education, by J.C. Agrawala, 1968, Doaba House, New Delhi.

Internet:

www.indusearlyyears.com

www.educationforallindia.com

www.unesco.org/new/en/education

en.wikipedia.org/wiki.

NOTES

1. Professor Mikko Ojala (1978a, 308-313) in his article ´Early Childhood Education as a Science´ maintained that early childhood education an activity that takes place before the school age. In this case preschool is a part of early childhood education. The aim of early childhood education is a versatile development of child´s personality. Besides education and teaching, early childhood education also includes a basic care. Early childhood education should help a child to be ready and mature for a smooth transfer to school. Ojala (1978a, 312) underlines that in education the theory should serve the practice and practice should serve the theory.
2. Learning (UNESCO; EFA Global Monitoring Report-2007). The term 'education' covers learning, a process of acquiring knowledge, skills, habits, and attitudes in order to prepare the young child to enter the formal education system.
3. Bombay Community Public Trust : Understanding the Cicic Issues of ECCE: The first six years of a child's life have been recognised as the most critical ones for optimal development. Since the process of human development is essentially cumulative in nature, investment in programmes for the youngest children in the range of 0-6 years has begun to be accepted as the very foundation for basic education and lifelong learning and development. Over the years, the field of childcare, inspired by research and front-line experiences, has

developed into a coherent vision for early childhood care and education.

4. NCERT; National Curriculum Framework-2005 Position Paper; National Focus Group on Early Childhood Care and Education.
5. Mishra R.C; Early Childhood Care and Education, 2005; APH Publishing Corporation.
6. Dr. M. Sakku Bhavya; Early Childhood Education, 2007.
7. 86th constitution amendment of Constitution of India in its Article-45 points about ECCE.
8. Constitution of India: ECCE is defined under DPSP chapter.
9. UDHR, 1948. Article-26.
10 Darkar Framework For Action-2000 (DFA).
11 B. Shiva Rao, Minutes of the Proceedings of Fundamental Rights Sub-Committee Meeting of March 27, 1947, pp. 124-126 and Sir Alladi Krishnaswami Ayyar.
12. Constituent Assembly Debate, Vol. II, 538-40)
13. National Policy on Education- 1968, Para 4(4)
14. National Policy on Education- 1986, Para 3.2
15. Reference to NPE- 1968 4 (1), " Strenuous efforts should be made for the early fulfillment of Directive Principle under Article-45 of the Constitution seeking to provide free and compulsory education for all children upto age of 14."
16. Acharya Ramamurti Committee Report, suprenote-5 at Para 6.1.2 & 6.1.3.
17. AIR 1992 SC, 1858.
18. (1993) 1 SCC, 645.
19. ibid , 476.
20. Granvile Austin; The Indian Constitution: Cornerstone of a Nation (1985), Oxford University Press, Bombay.
21. H.K Saharay; The Constitution of India: An Analytical Approach; 2nd. edition, 1997, 281.
22. Article–14; 'The State shall not deny to any person equality before law and the equal protection of the laws within the territory of India."

23. Article– 15 (1) 'The State shall not discriminate against any citizen on grounds of religion, race, caste, sex, place of birth or any of them."
24. Article –24 'No child below the age of fourteen years shall be employed to work in any factory or mine or engaged in any other hazardous employment."
25. List II- State List, Entry–11 (Omitted by the Constitution 42nd Amendment Act, 1976, Section 57.
26. List III - Concurrent List, Entry 25 reads as " Education, including technical education, medical education and universities, subject to the provisions of Entries 63, 64, 65, 66 of the List I; vocational and technical training of labour".
27. Darkar Framework of Action and is committed to achieve education for all by 2015.
28. Selected Educational Statistics- 2000-01.
29. According to a report of the Ministry of Human Resource Development, GOI, the GER in Primary Classes had gone up from 42.6 percent in 1950-51 to 95.7 percent in 2000-01 and in Upper Primary level, this had progressed to 58.8 percent in 2000-01 from 12.7 percent in 1950-51.The SES of 2005-06 shows that the GER is 111.24 in Primary Classes, 73.63 in Upper Primary Classes, and 96.92 in Elementary Stages (Classes I-VIII).
30. WCD Department, Government of India.
31. Ministry of HRD, Government of India.
32. NFHS Survey Repost.
33. SES- 2006-07.
34. Selected Educational Statistics- 2006-07, Ministry of HRD, GOI.
35. National Human Development Report-2001, prepared and published by the Planning Commission of India.
36. National Sample Survey Organization (NSSO), the National Human Development Report 36-2001.
37. Women & Men in India-2004, Central Statistical Organization, Ministry of Programme Implementation, GOI.
38. 11th Five-Year Plan, Government of India.

2

Early Childhood Care and Education in India: Origin and Background

The programme of Early Childhood Care and Education (ECCE) has been expanded in the world since 1990 following to the adoption of United Nations Convention on the Rights of the Child (UNCRC). Early Childhood Care and Education (ECCE) refers a comprehensive services intended for holistic development of the child before the age of six years. This is the period of his/her entry in to primary education. Here, the concept of care in the early childhood is the most critical element as it lays foundation for the all round growth and development of person's life. Considering the major importance of early childhood years, early childhood care is not left exclusively to parental/family care; rather it has been institutionalized. Since the adoption of Convention on the Rights of the Child in the United Nations General Assembly in 1989, a major transformation has been taken place in the lives of the World's a child as this Convention confers wide range of rights to the children for their survival, protection, development and participation.[1]

As far as ECCE is concerned, the Convention of the Rights of the child requires the State Parties to ensure to the maximum extent possible the survival and development of the child, to render appropriate assistance to parents and legal guardians in performance of their child-rearing responsibilities and ensure the development of institutions, facilities and services for the care of children. It also requires State Parties to take all appropriate measures to ensure that children of working parents have the right to benefit from child rearing services and facilities for which they are eligible. The Convention recognizes the link of the state of young child with the status and role of mother.

State of Early Childhood Care and Education in India

The development of children has been an integral part of national planning since 1951 and for which government of India has formulated policies, schemes and plan of action for children. References to early childhood care, development (holistic development), education (pre-primary education) are made in National Policy for Children (1974), National Policy for Education (1986), and National Plan of Action for Children (1992 & 2005), National Five-Year Plans, Integrated Child Development Services Schemes, Rajiv Gandhi National Crèche Scheme and Sarva Siksha Abhiyan. Here the national policies, programmes and schemes are reviewed that have direct or indirect bearing to early childhood care and education.

Definition of ECCE

The Early Childhood Care and Development is defined as the rights of the children in early childhood years (conception to completion of six years) for the survival, growth and optimum development, which requires holistic and integrated approach from the family, community and state in the right-based perspectives. Early Childhood Care and Education (ECCE) refers to programmes intended to provide care/and/or education for children until they complete six years of age, i.e. the period of their entry into primary education.

Objective of ECCE

Enhancing the quality of young children's lives is now a national and international priority. "Expanding and improving comprehensive early childhood care and education, especially for the most vulnerable and disadvantaged children" is number one goal of the Darkar Framework for Action (2000) on 'Education for All.' Early Childhood Care and Development (ECCD) programs helps to improve school performance as well as reduce dropout and repetition rate, which ultimately reduce cost and improve efficiency of primary education. It also has a long term impact on country's education, health, moral and social values and children's development as a whole. Early Childhood Development (ECD) emphasizes a holistic approach focusing on the child's physical, emotional, social as well as cognitive development. The objective of ECCE is to nurture the children for their physical and mental development and to prepare them for schooling with right attitudes and habits.[2]

Background on ECCE

The field of early childhood dates back to almost 150 years since the days of Plato and Aristotle in ancient Greek. In subsequent centuries, Europe became a rich source of early childhood advocates who stressed on the importance of a child's first seven years of life. The importance of educating poor children did not gain attention until the early 19th century when Robert Owen provided poor children with opportunities for education and societal improvements and Pestalozzi advocated teaching the whole child as well as poor children. As a result, conceptions of childhood changed from that of a miniature adult to that of a child with rights, the right to learn through play. New ways of teaching children emerged focusing on child development, appropriate curriculum and learning. In the 1960s, civil rights and women's rights movements impacted the nature of early childhood programmes and highlighted the importance of educating disadvantaged children. A host of factors such as industrialization, increased number of women with young children entering the labor force, families with two working parents, and the demise of traditional systems of child care and extended family support systems led to a growing demand for quality early childhood programmes.

ECCE Concept in India

By incorporating the provisions of the early childhood care and education in the constitutional provision of India, the law makers have acknowledged its importance of ECCE in great deal. Subsequently, all efforts have been made by the government in delivering the early childhood care and education service through ICDS. The 10th Five Year Plan have put enormous emphasis on early childhood care and education with special focus to strengthen pre-school component of ICDS and the 11th Five Year Plan has recommended for one year pre-school education for children before entering into primary schools. What concern is that the terminology of ECCE is not defined in the policy level? Since the elements of early childhood care and education are not delineated in the policy framework, different people understand the subject in different way. Lack of conceptual clarity is tended to create ambiguity even among the service delivery personnel.[3]

Unsatisfactory Progress

Integrated Child Development Services (ICDS) is the only flagship programme that looks for the holistic development of the young children. As a part of early childhood care and education, pre-school education is being provided to children under ICDS. Thus the subject of pre-primary education including the care of pre-school children has been transferred to the Ministry of Women and Child Development through an amendment to the Government of India. In order to comply the Supreme Court directives, government of India has putting efforts to universalize the ICDS service with expansion of anganwadis to all settlements and improving the quality of service.

However, the coverage of ICDS is still inadequate. As on today there were more than 13.5 lakh sanctioned anganwadis across the country against the minimum requirement 19 lakh. The unavailability of basic facilities at the anganwadis is also a major concern. A study conducted by National Council of Applied Economic Research revealed that around 40 per cent of AWCs were not housed in ICDS building nor in the rented building; more than 45 per cent of anganwadis did not have toilet facilities and 27 per cent anganwadis did not drinking water facilities.

Uncoonditional Linkage between Early Childhood Care and Pre-School Education

ICDS programme does not have the balance linkage between health, nutrition and pre-primary education. ICDS is a programme of basic health (i.e. immunization, health check-up) and supplementary feeding rather than a programme for early childhood education (i.e. pre-primary education). From policy approach to actual implementation, there are plenty of problems ICDS particularly related to pre-school activities. Pre-school education at Anganwadi centers is hampered largely due to –

1. Lack of basic infrastructure (i.e. building, space, playground & game materials, learning kits),
2. Untrained or inadequately trained pre-school instructor (AWW),
3. Absence of standard pre-school curriculum indicating learning methods for pre-school activities, language to be used for communication.
4. Lack of monitoring and supervision.
5. Absence of community participation.

Discrimination

Apart from government initiatives, private sectors, corporate bodies, and missionaries are also providing early childhood education in the form of kindergarten, nursery or pre-school education in a variety of modes and varying degree of quality. The children of rich families and elite classes can afford to receive high quality early childhood education, whereas children of poor and unprivileged families are either deprived of getting early childhood education or integrated with the ICDS that renders poor quality service. Children from advantaged families tend to arrive at schools with higher level of school readiness, advanced cognitive skills, and positive approach to learning. Conversely, children entering into schools without pre-primary education have lower level of motivation, cognitive skills and are more often faced with difficulties to cope with the school systems. While the syllabi and curriculum adopted by Public English Medium for pre-primary education have forward linkage with the primary education, ICDS sponsored pre-school education does not have such linkage.

ICDS Does Not Have School Readiness Programme

The importance of early childhood care and education for educational achievement in later years is internationally recognized and strongly evidenced in many research findings. Good beginnings of learning in early years in positive setting may ensure a smooth transition of from pre-school to primary school education. Hence, ECCE nurtures important dispositions and attitudes towards learning and positively supports educational achievements. Transition is a process and that starts from pre-school and continues until the child is established and coped with the formal education system in the primary level.

The successful transition from pre-school to primary school is overwhelmed with two separate but interconnected factors- "School Readiness" and "Ready Schools" The former stresses the role of ECCE in promoting children development and adapting them to the practice and environment of primary schools. School readiness includes development of 5 distinct but interconnected areas:

1) Child health and physical development;
2) Social and emotional development;
3) Approaches to learning (i.e. enthusiasm, curiosity, persistence)
4) Language and communication skills;
5) Cognitive development and Problem solving skills.

Ready school emphasizes the school adaptation to the child's development needs. It focuses on the accessibility of primary schools, quality environment, trained teachers, method driven teaching. Ideally the entire gamut of educational system should start with pre-primary education moves to highest ladder covering the primary elementary, and secondary education. Although the pre-primary education constitutes a part of ICDS component, it receives least importance. There is no structured curriculum and standardized norms for anganwadi workers to follow for pre-school education. The objective of early childhood care and education programme is to provide joyful learning environment and to follow play based learning activities in order to foster all round development of the child. However, it is observed that anganwadi workers tend to follow to formal learning method and give emphasis on reading, recitation and writing. Furthermore, Anganwadi center is not recognized as the pre-unit for child entry in primary education. The transition of the child to primary education is also not monitored at the anganwadi level.

A large number of women, particularly from low socio-economic strata, have to spend most of their time in earning livelihood. In these circumstances it becomes necessary to have ECCE programmes as an organized intervention to compensate the deprivations faced by young children whose mothers work outside the home. Here the creches' service is essentially felt. The evidence is growing that ECCE is the most effective area of intervention and it can be used to break the "cycle of deprivation". At each stage of the development span, every person is fully entitled to enjoy human rights. Children have rights too and the right to develop fully should be universally accepted.

Further, even the best of families cannot normally provide the kind of Stimulating play activities and the company of other children, that preschool is in a position to provide. There is a great advantage, joy as well, in collective activity, sharing, learning to wait, and enjoying doing things together with others. There are universal values of harmony with others, compassion for all living things and so on, which can easily be communicated to the children in the course of the ECCE programme.

The investment in child development in the early years, a child grows up and also becomes productive adults. Adults who are normally their caregivers can enter the labour market and improve their economic status considerably. Investment in children's early care has long term effects on their future as adults, saving social costs. For instance, children of deprived families who had quality child care have been found to show fewer instances of delinquency and drug addiction. In other words, investment in children during the critical period of the first six years will save the nation a great deal in terms of money and preservation of the social fabric.

Research finds that, about 80% of the personality characteristics observable in men or women develop during the early childhood years. According to the brain cells, which affect the whole life of a man or woman, are developed before the end of five years during early childhood. It has also been revealed that quality development of at about 60% of his intelligence is developed during these years. At the end of early childhood, a child will acquire language skills and also skills such as walking, jumping, playing and to live" alone" doing his work by himself. Accordingly the early childhood is significant as a critical stage, which cannot be compared to any other stage in life as it lays the foundation for aspects of human life.

As per the new research in the fields of education and psychology mal-nutrition, under-development and poor health contributes to backwardness in learning and low intelligence during formal schooling. Thus, it is barely essential to provide a child in the early childhood years not only the required nutrition and adequate health facilities but also care, love, protection, enthusiasm, pleasantness and a favorable social environment which are provided in the form of early childhood care and education. Early childhood is a period is a very influential period for the development of the child as well as for the development of a nation as a whole.[4] Various studies show that early childhood development can improve academic achievement and productivity in later period of life. Erickson who traced children' development from infancy to adulthood concluded that "childhood provides an early picture of an adult human being. Different behaviors in adults may be detected in childhood."

Psychologists are of the opinion that the pre-school development stages from the ages of 3 to 6 are the most important stage of all the development stages. It is at this stage that the foundation for the complex behavioral structure is laid. Children are an essential capital for the development of a nation's human resources. Neuro science research shows that the fastest development of human brain takes place within the first years of human life. Until the age of 4, a child's intelligence has developed by 50 per cent, and by the age of 8, it has increased to 80 per cent. Hence, the early childhood age is also called as the golden age. It is the stage of development when most of the brain cell tissues that control human activities and qualities are formed. As every development stage takes place only once in a life time, developmental deprivation in the golden age means a great loss of a lifetime. As a participant of the World Summit for Children (WSC) held by the United Nations on September 30, 1990.

Recent Trends in Early Childhood Care and Education

Since the 1980s, the Early Childhood Care and Education (ECCE) has been defined as the education of young children from birth to age of 6 years age. This wide age range has shown a growing debate and a lack of consensus as to what type of programme is most appropriate. Typically, ECCE programmes contain several age related areas ranging from infancy, pre-school, kindergarten and primary grades. Such programmes not only vary by age but by characteristics of the child in each stage, by purpose and by institutional sponsorship; they are offered in a variety of settings under diverse modes and wide practices.

Research findings on the short as well as long term outcomes of ECCE programmes have shown that children from low-income families who enrolled benefited a lot. Significant short term benefits were evident on children's Intelligence Quotient (IQ). As for long-term gains children were more successful in areas of school achievement. They were less likely to be retained and few of the children required special education services or placement. Some programmes have also been associated with positive outcomes in cognitive, social, and emotional development in children. These findings prompted governments and educators to begin investing their respective resources in the development and enhancement of learning opportunities for young children.

The international drive for expanding ECCE programmes began in 1989 with the adoption of the UN Convention on the Rights of the Child. This became evident when in 1990 at the World Conference on Education for All in Jomtien, Thailand, delegates from 155 countries, as well as representatives from some 150 organizations adopted the World Declaration on Education for All. In Article-5, it called for broadening the scope of basic education by recognizing that learning begins at birth. It also prioritized early childhood care and education (ECCE) as a foundation for later learning and development and called for early childhood care and initial education to be provided through a variety of arrangements involving families, communities or institutional programmes. This world conference helped the field of early childhood education find its way into policy-making agendas.

To advance the objective of EFA, a World Conference on Special Needs Education was held in Salamanca, Spain in 1994. Representatives from 92 governments and 25 international organizations called for inclusion to be part of early childhood care and education programmes for children aged up to six years and that it ought to be developed and reoriented to promote physical, intellectual and social development and school readiness. Later, the World Education Forum in Darkar 2000 which included 1,100 participants from 164 countries adopted the Dakar Framework for Action, reviewed the advances made in basic education in the 1990s, and strengthened the commitment to achieve quality basic education for all by 2015. In addition, it focused attention on the world's youngest children where they became a global agenda for EFA by 2000 through setting specific goals for them.

The first specific goal of the Dakar Framework for Action

called for expanding and improving comprehensive early childhood care and education, especially for the most vulnerable and disadvantaged children. Much of the concept of early childhood has been dominated by western values, beliefs and practices. It is, therefore, essential to consider the social context and the impact of different ideologies on education as well as the effect of political systems and structures on schooling systems when examining other countries. In addition, recent conceptual frameworks of child development and early childhood education have suggested that social class, gender, race, and culture are much ignored factors in the thinking and debate about child development and learnings. Whether ruled by an autocratic, democratic, or monarchical state, each society has its own beliefs about teaching children and ensuring that the values of the culture are passed to the next generation of children, thereby, shaping the representations of childhood, values, child rearing practices, family relationships and interactions.

Therefore, examining the social, political, demographic, and cultural context of countries provides important guidelines for a better understanding of the features, challenges, and prospects of early childhood programmes.

Early Childhood Education is a term that refers to educational programs and strategies geared toward children from birth to the age of six. This time period is widely considered the most vulnerable and crucial stage of a person's life. Early childhood education often focuses on guiding children to learn through play. The term often refers to preschool or infant/child care programs.

The New Education Policy of the Government of India, 1986

The New Education Policy of the Government of India, 1986, strongly emphasizes the importance of the early years of childhood, and the need for providing Early Childhood Care and Education (ECCE) services on a national scale, both to serve as a feeder into primary education and to enable women to join the workforce by providing quality services for the care of their children. One needs trained people with the right perspective about ECCE to work in a child care centre.[5]

The specific objectives of the Programme are to enable the learner:

- To develop an understanding about the needs and rights of children with emphasis on the socio-cultural context of childhood
- To understand the development of children from birth to six years of age;
- To plan play activities for fostering development;
- To appreciate the health and nutritional needs of young children and to be able to evaluate a diet as regards nutritional adequacy;
- To be able to identify common childhood illnesses, take care of the sick child and take preventive measures;
- To interact with the community and impart simple health, nutrition and preschool education and early childhood care and education massages;
- To identify children with special needs, be able to take care of their needs within the setting of the child care centre and take preventive action;
- To gain knowledge and develop skills and attitudes required for working with young children; and
- To set up, manage and work in child-care centers such as crèches, preschools, nursery schools, kindergartens and day care centres.

Integrated Child Development Services (ICDS)

Integrated Child Development Services as the largest government-managed programme at present in the country is an inter-sectoral programme which seeks to directly reach out to children from vulnerable and remote areas and give them a head-start by providing an integrated programme of health, nutrition and early childhood education. The package of services includes:

- Holistic development of the child; i.e. psycho-motor development, cognitive development, language development, social development.
- Prepares child for formal schooling.
- Intellectual development of child.
- Contributes in Universal Elementary Education.
- Health and Nutrition.
- Preparation for primary schooling.
- Reduces wastage and stagnation at primary school.

Research of behavioral and medical science confirms that early development of brain occurs primarily in the first few years of life, when foundation for a person's cognitive skill and learning capacity is laid. Good programmes of ECCE enhance physical growth and psycho-motor development, social and emotional development, language development and basic cognitive skills. This fact was well accepted in the World Declaration on Education for All (UNESCO, 1990) and in the Darkar Framework for Action, 2000, which sets target that all children should have access to good quality primary education by 2015, with particular attention to girls, ethnic minorities and disadvantaged children. The target also include expanding and improving the services of ECCE as it makes children ready for formal education, reduce delayed enrollment, and reduce dropout rate. It was also agreed that a holistic approach to the ECCE would be a stepping stone to achieve the target. Further, it is studied that malnutrition occurs in the first two years of life and after that this is irreversible. It is also well understood that a malnourished mother more often give birth to underweight child, who in turn grows up to a malnourished adolescent and in the case of girls, perpetuates the 'cycle of malnutrition' by giving birth to a low birth weight baby. Thus, programmes on ECCE are required to touch the key dimensions including, child health, child nutrition, child education, child development, and women health.[6]

The urgency for ECCE has been felt in India not only that India has ratified the Convention on the Rights of the Child or is a signatory to the Darkar Framework for Action, or is committed to the 'World Fit for Children' but also for reducing high infant and under-five mortality rate, malnutrition rate, improve female-male sex ratio and increase enrolment ratio as well as to reduce the dropout rate. Realizing its importance, ECCE has been incorporated in the Constitution of India in the year 2002 under the Directive Principles of State Policy, directing State to provide early childhood care and education for all children until they complete the age of six years. Despite the constitutional recognition to early childhood rights, the state of early childhood care and development remains the same as it was before 86th Constitutional Amendment Act (2002) making ECCE as the responsibility of the State.

As per the framework of the Constitution of India, the provisions contained in the Directive Principles of State Policy shall not be enforceable in court of law; but the principles are nevertheless fundamental in the governance of the country and it shall be duty of the State to apply these principles in making the laws. The hopes and aspirations of the people get translated under the directive principles of state policy. The law making power of the State is guided by the DPSP. What is fuming that no law has been made on ECCE despite its entry in this part of the Constitution.

Early childhood is defined as the period from birth to Six years old. A time of remarkable brain growth, these years laid the foundation for subsequent learning and development. UNESCO advocates for Early Childhood Care and Education (ECCE) programmes that attend to health, nutrition, security and learning and which provide for children's holistic development. It organized the first World Conference on ECCE in September 2010, which culminated in the adoption of a global action agenda for ECCE called Moscow Framework for Action and Cooperation: Harnessing the Wealth of Nations. As a follow-up to the World Conference, UNESCO works in partnership with Member States, partners and other stakeholders to encourage timely and effective implementation of the Moscow Framework so that all young children develop their potential to the fullest.

Various studies have shown that early childhood development can improve academic achievement and productivity in the later period of life. Erickson who traced children's development from infancy to adulthood concluded that "childhood provides an early picture of an adult human being. Different behaviors in adults may be detected in childhood." Psychologists are of the opinion that pre-school development stage from the ages of 2 to 5 years of age and this is the most important stage of all the development stages. This is the stage that laid the foundation for the complex behavioral structure.

Children are an essential capital for the development of a nation's human resources. Neuro science research shows that the fastest development of human brain takes place within the first years of human life. Until the age of 4, a child's intelligence has developed by 50 per cent, and by the age of 8, it has increased up to 80 per cent. Hence, the early childhood age is also called the golden age as most of the brain cell tissues that control human activities and qualities are formed. As every development stage takes place only once in a life time, developmental deprivation in the golden age means a great loss of a lifetime. As a participant of the World Summit for Children (WSC) held by the United Nations on September 30, 1990.

Childhood is a state of wonder - a time when the world is fresh and every event is interesting for him. Suppose, an ants crawling on the floor, a cat jumping from the wall, the sound of water dripping from a tap - each of these is a fascination for the every young child. The child is born without fear and with a wide-eyed interest in the people and things around him. It is therefore becomes very important that the family should nurture the the child carefully in helping her for a strong emotional bonds with parents and others, to realise her potential and to be a healthy individual physically, mentally and socially. Care and protection is very much essential for the survival of the infant. The continued affectionate attention for the the child needs in the early years as it is important for the child to thrive and to grow up into a happy adulthood. The argument for investing in early childhood development has been stated convincingly by several people and in different ways. Recognizing the holistic nature of child development, viz, nutrition, health and social, mental, physical, moral and emotional development, Early Childhood Care and Education (ECCE) will receive high priority. Thus the Pogrmmes of ECCE should be child-oriented and focused around play and the individuality of the child.

Theory and Practice of Early Childhood Care and Education

Whatever its political ideology, system it may be, no nation today can't afford to ignore the establishment of social justice, human rights and equality. The early childhood care is a measure of ensuring equity, both socio-economic and gender related. The early childhood care is such an overwhelming concept need felt by the families that any attempt to provide it along with other programmes for women, such as income generating schemes, is bound to be a success. For instance, in rural development schemes, where women come to upgrade their skills or to work, an added child development programme strengthens all fronts.[7] Similarly, primary schools, which attach a section for the under-sixes, find that school attendance of older children, especially girls, improves while also ensuring that pre-school age children are in a safe and stimulating environment.[8] Today, around the world, family structures have changed. There are very few joint families. There are also single parent families and a substantive number of women-headed families. Furthermore, migration constantly alters the demographic patterns – throwing men into cities, sometimes with and sometimes without their families. Apart from rural to urban migration, common all over the world as populations are getting rapidly urbanized, there is regional migration. For many of these reasons, a substantial investment in early childhood development programmes is an absolute necessity. Thus we see that from several points of view such as human rights, moral values, social equity and economic gains, early childhood development makes for the best investment. Having accepted the several reasons in favor of ECCE, what are the steps to be taken by policy makers? What should be done? In the next Section we will look into this aspect, taking into consideration some of the important issues involved.

The development of the child is not only concerned with what is happening within the child, but also to the care that the child requires. It is imperative that the basic needs like protection, food and health care is also important for the child is equally important to meet the child's needs for affection and security, for stimulation and interaction. Thus meeting the health and nutritional needs of the child is of course an essential prerequisite for optimum development of the child. Fostering a healthy foundation includes measures like improving maternal health, educating the mother and other caregivers about the importance of breast feeding, irnmunisation, supplementary feeding and growth monitoring etc.[9]

In addition to catering to the health and nutritional needs and providing physical care to the child, it is also important to provide stimulation also. So, the early childhood stimulation attempts to provide learning opportunities to the child so as to enhance her development. However, the learning experiences need to be so planned that they are in accordance with the child's maturational status.

This stimulation should be provided from early infancy by and large, stimulation comprises activities that involve a close interaction between the child and the caregiver. The basis of these activities is a warm, loving relationship between the child and the care giver. Thus, an affectionate and aware caregiver holds the key to the child's optimum development. It is important that the trained ECCE worker instills this confidence in individual parents that even if they are poor and illiterate, they can provide stimulation to their child, and that it should be done right from early infancy. Thus, not only family members, but also workers in preschool centers (be it the Balwadi, Anganwadi, a nursery school or an early childhood education i.e. ECE centre), who have to be educated regarding how stimulation should be provided to the young children.

There is research evidence built over a period of time, in a variety of settings from which the following facts are derived:

- Development and learning occur as children interact with people and objects.
- A healthy environment, space, materials and time for play as well as adults who foster learning and nurture relationships - these are the essentials.
- Children need to be actively involved in order to learn.
- Opportunities for them to play and try out things should be provided.
- A holistic approach to the child's development must be taken.
- Physical, mental, 'socio-emotional aspects being inter-related, anything that happens to the child affects everything else.

Giving due cognizance to these and similar findings, it is now universally agreed that it is necessary to have ECCE programmes and that these must be holistic in nature. Recognizing and catering to the specific developmental needs of younger children, these programmes will increase the general awareness of the value of a commitment to children and will enable the community to reach its youngest citizens in a meaningful way.

Childhood education often focuses on children learning through play, based on the research and philosophy of Jean Piaget. This belief is centered on the "power of play". It has been thought that children learn more efficiently and gain more knowledge through play-based activities such as dramatic play, art and social games. This theory plays stems children's natural curiosity and tendencies to "make believe", mixing in educational lessons. Pre-school education and kindergarten emphasize learning around the ages of 3-6 years. The terms "day care" and "child care" do not convey the educational aspects, although many childcare centers are now using more educational approaches.

The distinction between childcare centers and kindergartens has all but disappeared in countries that require staff in different early childhood facilities to have a teaching qualification. Researchers and early childhood educators both view the parents as an integral part of the early childhood education process.[2] Often educators refer to parents as the child's "first and best teacher". Much of the first two years of life are spent in the creation of a child's first "sense of self"; most children are able to differentiate between themselves and others by their second year. This is a crucial part of the child's ability to determine how they should function in relation to other people.[3] Early care must emphasize links to family, home culture, and home language by uniquely caring for each child.

Children who lack sufficient nurturing, nutrition, interaction with a parent or caregiver, and stimulus during this crucial period may be left with developmental deficits, as has been reported in Russian and Romanian orphanages.[4] Children must receive attention and affection to develop in a healthy manner. There is a false belief that more hours of formal education for a very young child confers greater benefits than a balance between formal education and family time. A systematic, international review suggests that the benefits of early childhood education come from the experience of participation; more than 2.5 hours a day does not greatly add to child development outcomes, especially when it detracts from other experiences and family contact.

National Early Childhood Care & Education, New Delhi (NECCE) was legally established under the guidance of eminent jurist's educationists and Social Workers for the development of Education under IT Act 1882. The same is organized by Radhika Educational & Social Welfare Trust, New Delhi for propagation and development of education on NCERT pattern.

Objectives

Delivering education at the door steps of the candidates at distant places;

- To provide job-oriented and professional courses for youth enabling them for getting suitable employments.
- To promote education under Open & Distance Education System on the international pattern for near & remote areas as well.
- To train skilled teachers in latest technology application for daily life.
- To train candidates in State of Art Technologies of Teaching & Guidance.
- To enable youth to be productive and useful citizen in the fast changing globalization of the world.

What Parents Must Look for in an ECCE Centre

New research that has focused on the need for integrated interventions addressing child survival, growth and development has noted the impact of health and nutrition status, early stimulation on brain development, importance of early socialization patterns and the quality of the child's immediate environment. These factors critically influence the child's physical, cognitive, emotional and social development in later life. Brain development patterns suggest that learning opportunities in the environment have a dramatic and specific effect, not merely influencing the general direction of development, but also affecting how the brain functions.

Addressing 'quality' the aspects of ECCE has not yet received the required attention, while the focus continues to remain largely on 'achieving quantitative target figures'. The balance between quality and quantity is more precarious than ever. Indeed, the competing challenges of quantitative outreach vis-à-vis quality dimensions are not easy to overcome but there is urgent and imperative need to appreciate that a balanced approach is crucial.

The centers, which are expected at best to provide necessary maturational and experiential readiness to the child, have been turned into regular sessions for training children that admission to primary schools would otherwise be denied. Thus, what should have been a simple pre-preparatory environment for creating interest and readiness for learning becomes a rigorous pressurizing and premature exercise for performance and achievement. Parents need to be aware of the damage created by such pressures on young children. Many issues and concerns confront parents in the selection of an appropriate ECCE centre for their children. At present, in the absence of the system of licensing.

Early Childhood Education Issues

Educationalists and psychologists agree that it is within the first six years that the foundations of an individual's linguistic, cognitive, social, creative, physical, moral and spiritual development evolve.[10] To help achieve its goals of facilitating professional development and public understanding of early childhood education, NAEYC identifies and addresses the issues that shape the field. The case for educational provision before the commencement of formal education at five or six years of age has received support from a wide range of research findings including those of Hebb and McGill.[11]

- Supplementary Nutrition,
- Immunization,
- Health checkups,
- Referral services,
- Non-formal pre-school education.

Nutrition and health education for children below six years and pregnant and nursing mothers. What should be done: We should reach at the children and their families who are most in need. At present there are, in many countries, early childhood education schemes for fee paying children. But the real challenge is to identify the children at risk and to plan suitable interventions for them. Given the population of India and the magnitude of poverty, the number of needy children in the 0-6 year age group is very large indeed. Though the issue of large scale quantitative expansion of ECCE facilities to reach the maximum number of these children is important, the issue of quality of ECCE services provided is as important, particularly in view of the existing limitations of funds and facilities. To what extent is it possible to reduce the cost of an ECCE programme in order to reach the largest proportion of the target population while maintaining a good quality? In this context, experts are of the opinion that when inputs go below a critical minimum, the affectivity is lost and the programme fails to fulfil its objectives. Therefore, while quantitative expansion of ECCE programmes is important, the issue of making these programmes qualitatively effective through measures such as adequate and appropriate training of personnel and provision of sufficient and suitable materials and facilities is crucial, and needs attention. Even though the families of the at-risk children identified may not have formal education, we should not assume that they are ignorant. We should involve them in deciding what to offer to their children and how to monitor it. In this way, we would at least be sure that our programmes are culturally sensitive, and therefore can be sustained within the community. It is known that the first two years of a child's life are very important, and yet many of our schemes tend not to include them. Among the tasks that need to be do is that of providing holistic care for infants, be the programmes centre based or home based.

Why ECCE is Important

While the Right to Free and Compulsory Education Act, 2009, ensures that education is a fundamental right of every child between six and 14 years, it seems to overlook the vital needs of early childhood care and education. However, contemporary research establishes the fact that a child's brain grows at an extraordinary pace in the first six years of his/her life and lays the foundation for lifelong development. The experiences that a child draws from his surroundings contribute significantly to the formation of the synaptic connections in the brain.

The first six years of a child's life have been recognised as the most critical ones for optimal development. Since the process of human development is essentially cumulative in nature, investment in programmes for the youngest children in the range of 0-6 years has begun to be accepted as the very foundation for basic education and lifelong learning and development. Over the years, the field of childcare, inspired by research and front-line experiences, has developed into a coherent vision for early childhood care and education. It is now undisputedly acknowledged that the systematic provision of Early Childhood Care and Education (ECCE) helps in the development of children in a variety of ways. These include:

- Improving group socialisation,
- Inculcation of healthy habits,
- Stimulation of creative learning processes, and
- Enhanced scope for overall personality development.

Thus, ECCE must be promoted as holistic input for fostering psycho-social, nutritional, health and educational development of young children. For children belonging to under privileged groups and for first-generation learners in the society, ECCE is essential for countering the physical, intellectual and emotional deprivation of the child. From the perspective of the community, ECCE is a support for the universalisation of elementary education, and also indirectly influences enrolment and retention of girls in primary schools by providing substitute care facilities for younger siblings. ECCE is also envisaged in the role of a support service for working women.

The pre-school education component of ECCE has demonstrated a positive impact on retention rates and achievement levels in primary grades. However, it is important to note that attendance in pre-schools does not automatically guarantee better academic achievement. 'Quality' aspects, such as a healthy environment, stimulating activities and encouraging, care-giving teachers, are imperative to ensure all-round development in children. There is sufficient evidence to indicate that early childhood represents the best opportunity for breaking the inter-generational cycle of multiple disadvantages-chronic under-nutrition, poor health, gender discrimination and low socio-economic status.

Early childhood care and education should meet the child's need for protection, food and health care, along with the need for affection, security and stimulation and learning opportunities. Good early childhood care ensures that children will realise their full development potential and grow into productive adults. Early childhood care and education has become a very pertinent issue, given the research findings pertaining to the importance of early childhood years, the fact that effects of poverty and. deprivation can be compensated by early interventions, and given factors like changing family structure from joint to nuclear families, migration and an increasing number of women going out of the house to take up icds. It is essential that every country should provide good care to its children in the early ages not only for economic reasons, but also as a matter of social justice and human rights, since every child has a right to be looked after properly. The programmes of early childhood care and education should be holistic in nature rather than providing nutrition, health and education services piece-meal services. There are a number of these programmes being run in our country as well as in other developing countries. It is important to learn not only from one's own experience, but also from that of the others.

Justification for Government Intervention in ECCE

Across continents and nations, we see two main types of argument deployed to justify government intervention in early childhood care and education. These may be categorized as 'intrinsic' arguments and 'instrumentalist' arguments.

Arguments

Intrinsic arguments focus on children's inherent rights to develop their potential and the inescapable obligation falling on states to assist and promote children's development through the provision of services to them and to their parents. Discourse based on intrinsic arguments sees the UN Charter on the Rights of the Child as fundamental.

Intrinsic arguments are often used to press governments for comprehensive action on children's services, stressing the need for universal services, the indivisibility of the child's development needs, and the importance of integrated and comprehensive provision. Intrinsic arguments frequently stress the interdependence of early childhood education and childcare.[12]

However, appeals to human rights arguments do not necessarily persuade governments to take legislative action across the board to support ECCE. If governments accept human rights arguments, they are frequently selective about the rights they are prepared to enshrine in legislation. Pragmatic and economic considerations explain this, the cost of granting universal rights to ECCE is immense; and many governments are approaching this area of welfare provision incrementally, focusing first on what they consider the most fundamental rights. For many states, the right to early education comes first in terms of a universal entitlement, not least since it supports and strengthens the universal right to school education, which is very widely recognized.

Intrinsic arguments also have to cope with the fact that international human rights instruments are generally cast in broad and general terms, calling for example on states to develop a 'legal and policy framework' for ECCE. This is not the same thing as insisting on universal and enforceable rights to the full range of ECCE services. The UN Committee on the Rights of the Child recognizes that universal access to extensive services is a long term goal which must – as a matter of practical politics – be approached progressively.

Intrinsic arguments do however provide powerful backing to calls for integrated policy making and for a strategic approach to services, even if those services cannot immediately be universalized or cast as citizen's rights. As we have seen, many states have developed comprehensive strategies for early childhood services and, within those, have identified some services as universal and others as targeted on the children and families who are most vulnerable or disadvantaged.

Intrinsic, human rights-based arguments also stress the importance of equitable access to services for all children; of provision without discrimination; and of quality standards to ensure consistently good services for all children. It appeals to the results of government intervention in ECCE. They point to the gains – in terms of social cohesiveness, improved performance at school, enhanced cognitive functioning throughout life, greater capacity to acquire and use skills in the workplace – that investment in early childhood services yields. These arguments may be broadly termed 'return on human capital' lines of reasoning. They say, in effect, that investment in early childhood services makes good economic sense for states, since in the long term they will reap large rewards in terms of having a more skilled and versatile workforce and citizens who are well-adjusted, emotionally and socially.

The evidence to back instrumentalist arguments is extensive and weighty and has clearly influenced many states towards substantial investment in ECCE. In particular, the work of Heckman (in the US) and Melhuish (in the UK and elsewhere) has had extensive international exposure. Many studies in the field of neuroscience which offer instrumentalist support to ECCE examine early childhood brain development and point to the benefits in terms of mental functioning, emotional development, social adjustment and general wellbeing associated with appropriate childcare and early education. [13]

Another important strand of instrumentalist argument concerns social integration, the overcoming of social inequalities, and the promotion of inclusive communities. Some studies have shown how children, particularly from disadvantaged backgrounds, perform better at school and also in terms of their wider social adjustment and fulfillment in later life if they have had access to good quality early childhood services. Such evidence offers a powerful incentive to governments.

Again, however, governments have to grapple with the issue of priorities – if they cannot resource the totality of ECCE services on a universal basis, which services do they prioritize, and how do they defend their choice? We have seen from the international comparisons that many countries listen and act on instrumental arguments for universal pre-school education. They seem to have accepted the argument that, in the long run, the all-round benefits of universal provision of early education exceed the costs. So far as childcare and family support services are concerned, many states interpret the research evidence as pointing to the need to focus their limited resources on the most disadvantaged and excluded children and families.

Need-Based Approach

The ECCE in the form of child care, health care, pre-school education, and supplementary nutrition feeding is being given through ICDS Scheme, Rajiv Gandhi National Crèche Scheme, and SSA Programme. These are merely schemes and its execution rests on the moral precepts and political will of the government. Thus ECCE, in the present context, is considered as vital need of the child rather than a right. Even if the lawmakers have recognized ECCE as a contributory factor for realization right to education, the opportunity for services are fragmented and varied in quality. The above-mentioned points make it clear that the subject of early childhood care and education is not yet addressed in right-based perspective even though this has been incorporated in the Constitution since 2002.Whatever the services being offered through ICDS are not universal and more importantly these services lack quality. Thus, the immediate concern of the government to provide equal, indiscriminate, and quality ECCE service to all children.

Unequal Access & Transition Experience

Various service providers in the private sector (companies, private schools, missionaries) are providing early childhood education (in the form of kindergarten, nursery or pre-school).

The quality is variable. The children of high-income parents can buy access to pre-school education, though the purchase does not always guarantee quality provision. The children of poor and disadvantaged families either have no pre-school education at all or have to make do with a generally poor service as part of ICDS. Where provision is of a high standard, children arrive at primary school with advanced cognitive skills and a positive approach to learning. Where children have been exposed to no pre-primary provision, or provision of poor quality, they start school less able to make a smooth transition (especially where the primary school is not expert in dealing with the diversity of children's pre-primary experience and adopts too formal a style in the early grades).

ICDS does not have any explicit programme to help children prepare for school. By 'prepare for school', we do not refer to the kind of attempts made in some private institutions to advance the primary school curriculum or subject children to formal teaching methods, but to the gentle introduction of positive attitudes towards learning. There are no formal linkages between ICDS centers and primary schools that enable children to be prepared – and which would encourage schools to be 'ready for children'.

Gaps in Quality Assurance and Accountability

Pre-primary education is the neglected component of ICDS, receiving least attention. There is little appreciation of the need for play-based and informal learning: Anganwadi workers tend to follow a formal learning method and emphasis on reading, recitation and writing.

ICDS was conceived as a welfare scheme, catering for the needs of the most disadvantaged. Even as it is expanded, the philosophy is need-based, not rights-based. As a scheme, without statutory backing, it gives users no entitlements to service – even though the incorporation of ECCE within the 2002 Act signals that legislators recognize early education as an enabler for the right to school education. Where ECCE is wholly a matter of 'schemes', there is no certainty for citizens about access to services. They receive benefits, not their legal entitlement. Schemes are optional–governments can implement them or withdraw them as they choose, whereas entitlements, enshrined in legislation, are binding on governments. If entitlements are infringed or withheld, the citizens can use the law to challenge government and enforce performance.

Demand for the Legal Framework on ECCE

In order to promote early childhood programs and their quality, it is necessary to provide a legal framework of standards and norms that serve as the foundation of those progammes. Based on this framework, there will be increased accountability of the government and more financial allocation for implementation of the programmers. Here is provided some arguments for why legal framework is necessary as a statutory support to Article-45 of the Constitution of India.

First argument is that early childhood care and education is a core issue of human development. Early years of children lives are a time of tremendous opportunity for stimulating brain growth and development. Worldwide researches have claimed that early exposure to learning experiences in a stimulating environment will lead children to perform better in primary schools.

The second argument is based on India's obligation to international convention such as the United Nations Convention on the Rights of the Child, United Nations Declaration on Education for All, and Darkar Action Framework. The UNCRC affirms children right to Survival, Development, Protection, and Participation. The Education for All Declarations at Jometin in 1990, and Dakar in 2000 recognizes that children are born with the right to learning. These international doctrines have recognized early childhood care, education and development as the right of children.[14]

Further, the UN Committee on the Rights of the Child had gone a step ahead by interpreting every child's right to education as beginning at birth and closely tied to right to development, as spelt out in Article 6.2 of the UNCRC.[15] The Committee also recommends that States Parties shall pay greater attention to, and actively support, a right-based approach to early childhood programs. The Committee calls on States Parties to provide a legislative framework for the provision of quality, adequately resourced services. As India is the state party to the Convention, it is the responsibly of the government of India to comply the general recommendation of the Committee.

Thirdly, ECCE in the present policy context is not seen as a right of the child. Whatever the policies and schemes made by the government for addressing ECCE are largely based on humanitarian approach but not as a constitutional mandate. The basic difference between the law and scheme is that the former mandates the State to implement it, whereas the execution of the latter is obligatory for the state. Law usually permits a protective mechanism and violation of law by the State challenged in the Court of Law, on the contrary a policy or scheme lacks such. Law is made by the legislature and is amended by the legislature. The policy and schemes are just like executive made law and the executive at any point of time can abdicate these policies as per their conveniences. On the other hand, a law is enforceable in the court of law.

Fourthly, early childhood care and education need to be addressed from the perspective of educational development plan. The importance of early childhood care and education as the foundation of the pyramid of education system has accorded priority in India in the National Policy for Education (NPE), 1986 and the Programme of Action (POA) drew in 1992 for implementation of the NPE. The NPE viewed ECCE as crucial input as the strategy for human resource development, and a feeder and support programme for primary education. In the policy framework, for the first time NPE put enormous importance to early childhood care and education with the proposition that child's capacity for learning at primary level depends on past learning in the pre-primary level. Although subject ECCE has been incorporated in the constitution by virtue of 86th amendment, it does not mandate the government to act upon it. The directive, under Article-45, "State shall endeavour to provide early childhood care and education…." is only a direction and not subject to judicial scrutiny if State fails to comply this constitutional obligation. It was hoped that government would formulate a policy/legal framework on ECCE with an objective to translate the constitutional direction in a right-based approach. No substantial improvements are made so far in delivering of ECCE service even though a good number of years have passed since the insertion of early childhood care and education in the framework of constitution. Even though the importance of early childhood care and education (Pre-school education) is recognized in Section-11 of the Right of Children to Free and Compulsory Education Act, 2009, there is no hints of reference of service delivery systems of ECCE.

Fifthly, the provisions contained in the directive principles require statutory support. The Directive Principles of State Policy are guiding principles for the central and state governments of India to follow while framing laws and policies. Many of the provisions of the directives principles have been supported by legal framework. Few of these include, The Minimum Wages Act and Equal Remuneration Act, The National Rural Employment Guarantee Act for Article-39 relating to right to work, right to adequate means of livelihood, equal pay for equal work for both men and women; The Maternity Benefit Act to give effect to Article-42 that directs the state to have provision for securing just and humane conditions of work and maternity relief. The Legal Services Authority Act for Article-39 (A) dealing with equal justice and free legal aid; The Protection of Environment and Wildlife Act to give effect to Article-48 (A) concern with protection and improvement of environment and safeguarding of forest and wildlife.

In view of the foregoing discussions, the following broad principles and approaches should be taken into account.

- Adopting Right Based Approach,
- Defining ECCE in order to remove the ambiguities between early childhood care, early childhood education, and early childhood care and education.
- Laying down the duties of central government, state government and local self-government for delivering the service.
- Explaining the type of activities to be conducted.
- Prescribing standardized norms and guidelines for service delivery mechanisms, early childhood education curriculum.
- Prescribing standards regarding infrastructure, and programme quality.
- Laying down the provisions for recruitment, training, and orientation of staffs for human resource development.
- Prescribing norms for allocation of funds.
- Adopting integrated approach for coordination, convergence, and accountability.
- Prescribing guidelines for formation of management committee, community participation as well as for monitoring and evaluation of programme.
- Prescribing procedure for redressing of complaint.

Against this background – the arguments for state intervention in ECCE and specifically in early education and the gaps and shortcomings in provision in India. It is submitted that the immediate concern of the government should be to develop a strategic and over-arching policy framework for early childhood services and, within that, to grant all children a legally enforceable right to access high quality pre-school education.

References

1. A Study for Urban childhood programmes by Dr. Vrinda Datta, Tata Institute of Social Sciences.
2. Annual Report: Ministry of Women & Child Development; Government of India.
3. Care & Protection of Young Children under J.J. Act (2000).

4. Census of India (2011).
5. Children with parental Care, A CLAP Publication, Dr. Bikash Das.
6. DAV Institute of In Service Education Research.
7. Early Childhood matters, BVLF, Neitherland.
8. Early childhood Matters' Critical thinkings, Bernad Vanleer Foundation.
9. Early Years children- Promote health, case studies on child to child and Early Care and Development-The child to child trust childhood care and Education.
10. Education for All by 2015, will we make it, UNICEF Report.
11. Education watches Orissa, Citizens report on quality elementary education-2006.
12. Ensuring children their childhood, V.V. Giri National Labour Institute, New Delhi.
13. Exploring the Rights of the Child in Early childhood, A CLAP Publication..
14. National Coordination Forum Education for All 2003.
15. National Family Health Survey Report.
16. Rajiv Gandhi National Crèche Scheme for the Children of Working/ Ailing Mothers.
17. RTE Act, 2009 and State Rules.
18. UNESCO: Education for All Global Monitoring Report (2007).
19. UNICEF: Progress for Children; A World Fit for Children Statistical Review (Number 6, December 2007).
20. United Nations Convention on the Rights of the Child.
21. United Nations Educationally Scientific and Cultural Organisation.
22. Walter Barker: Early Childhood Care & Education: The Challenge; Bernard van Leer Foundation.
23. www.ignou.ac.in/school/soce/org.
24. www.kidzee.com
25. www.oldweb.naeyc.org/ece

26. www.smilefoundationindia.org
27. www.sporoorti.org/children_education
28. www.unesco.org/new/eneducation.
29. www.wiseearch.com/earlychildhood.

Notes

1. United Nations Committee on the Rights of the Child Day of General Discussion on 'Implementing Child Rights in Early Childhood' 17 September 2004.
2. http://wikieducator.org/Early_childhood_care_and_development
3. Early Childhood Care and Education: Indian Perspective Dr Sheeranjan & Archana Sharma Awathi, World Conference on Early Childhood Care and Education.
4. Campaignforeducationusa.org: Global Campaign for Education, United States Chapter.
5. http://deta.qld.gov.au/earlychildhood/office/national/definitions.html
6. http://www.education.com/reference/article/Ref_What_Early_Childhood/
7. Care and Education in Early Childhood: A Student's Guide to Theory and Practice: Audrey urtis, Maureen O'Hagan.: www.questia.com/library/education/early-childhood.jsp
8. Trade in Care and Education in Early Childhood: A Student's Guide to Theory and Practice for an Amazon.co.uk
9. Care and Education in Early Childhood: A Student's Guide to Theory and Practice, Audrey Curtis, Maureen O'Hagan, edn. Illustrated, RoutledgeFalmer, 2003.
10. INTO Publication, Early Childhood Education Issues: Educationalists and psychologists agree that it is within the first six years that the foundations of an individual's linguistic, cognitive, social, creative, physical, moral and spiritual development evolve. Deficits in these areas of development can have long term implications for the child, often affecting his or her ability to respond to the challenges provided in the educational system. We owe it to

all young children to assist them in maximizing their individual potential. There would be much less need for remedial and compensatory education if resources were targeted at young children.

11. They are supported by findings of analyses of longitudinal studies of the development of children which showed a high correlation between the performances of children on general ability tests at four or five years of age and at seventeen years of age (Hunt 1961, Bloom 1964). Bloom observed that in terms of mental V Hunt Research on ECCE: (Hunt 1961, Bloom 1964) Development 50% takes place between 0-4 years, 30% takes place between 4-8 years, 20% takes place between 8-17 years.
12. NCER: National Campaign for Early Childhood Care and Education, Committee for Legal Aid to Poor.
13. The Hindu, New Delhi, March 26, 2012 Early Childhood Care and Education Policy proposed.
14. United Nations Declaration on Education For All, and Dakar Action Framework. The UNCRC affirms children right to Survival, Development, Protection, and Participation. The Education For All Declarations at Jometin in 1990, and Dakar in 2000.
15. A Guide to General Comment 7: Implementing child rights in early childhood (2006) by the UN Committee on the Rights of the Child, UNICEF

3

Early Childhood Care and Education in India and Other Countries

Man born, grows slowly, gets maturity and died, is the law of nature and no one is exception to this universal rule. The life starts from cradle and ends in the death of the individual. In fact human development starts from the period of conception and in early childhood period many development takes place with human being. The early childhood period as a very crucial stage that leads to all round development of the child. It also laid the foundation pillar for the path for the successful completion of primary education. Early childhood care and education inculcates fuel for the successful transition of child from pre-school environment to primary school education.

Early childhood is an important stage which prepares the child to a stage of readiness for the formal education. It also stimulates a feeling of interest in the child for education. Therefore the early childhood care and education leads towards the psycho social, nutritional, health, and educational development of the child. The quality of early childhood care and education can be developed through the provision of access like infrastructures, equipments, materials and others. The five components and dimension of ECCE are developmentally appropriate curriculum, trained teachers, appropriate teacher-child ratio and group size. Infra structure supportive to children's needs and encouraging style of supervisions.

The significance of early childhood care and education for country's education development is reiterated in international documents adopted in 1990s.[1] The sequence of international framework was began with the adoption of the Convention on the Rights of the Child by the United Nations on November 20, 1989. That was the first global document which set the international standards for the realization of children's rights in a right-based approach. As far as global commitment to education is concerned, the famous declaration 'learning begins at birth' adopted in the World Conference on Education for All (EFA) held at Jomtien of Thailand in March 1990, followed by World Education Forum held in 2000 at Darkar of Senegal are the two major international developments that have had great influence on countries' education policies. Since 1990, major developments have evolved across the world in the context of;

1. Expansion of early childhood programmes.
2. Increased debate on the role of ECCE and attitudes towards learning or supporting educational achievements.
3. Increased attention on the role of government to ensure the successful completion of primary education of all children.[2]

ECCE provides an important foundation for later learning of the children and also playing an integral part of lifelong learning. Good quality of early childhood care and education provision can equip the children with cognitive, behavioral, and social skills that generate large benefits in terms of access to primary school, progression through school and learning outcomes.[3] There are few cross-country research studies[4] that offer evidence of the benefits of early childhood education for educational indicators in terms of school readiness, increased enrolment, promoting learning achievement of child, and increased retention. Globally, the fundamental importance of early childhood care and education for child development and educational achievement has been at the forefront of discussion. Early childhood care and education has, of course, become a major subject of policy development and statutory provision in many countries of the world in reference to the Education for All (EFA) Global Monitoring Report-2009, it is understood that world wide access to ECCE facilities has been increasing.

Published statistics show that the worldwide enrolment of children in pre-school programme at worldwide grew from 139 million in 2006 from 112 million in 1999. However, there was a large disparity in growth rates as between developed and developing countries. There are also marked disparities for pre-primary education among the countries and regions. In 2006, the pre-primary gross enrolment ratio was 79% in developed countries as against 36% in developing countries. Coverage was lowest in Sub-Saharan Africa (14%) and the Arab States (18%). In 2006, the pre-primary GER was 44% in East Asia and 39% in South-West Asia to which world's two most populous country, China and India, belong respectively.[5]

Research in India also provides an evidence of effect of early childhood care and education programme on enrollment levels and academic preparedness of children for formal schooling. A longitudinal-cum-cross sectional study conducted by NCERT in eight States (Maharashtra, Rajasthan, Karnataka, Bihar, Tamil Nadu, Madhya Pradesh, Uttar Pradesh and Goa) indicate distinctly better rates of retention in children with ECE experience as compared to those who have sought direct entry in Grade-I. Further, the findings of National Evaluation of ECE programmes of ICDS conducted indicated the positive role played by early childhood education in promoting enrolment, retention in dropout and greater retention in primary schooling.[6]

This chapter illustrates how far India has progressed to ensure Early Childhood Care and Education in terms of EFA goal in a comparative perspective with other countries. It also briefly introduces the policy concepts underlying early childhood care and education and the availability of institutional facilities for deliverance of ECCE service. At the same time an attempt is made to summaries in plain terms the policy approaches taken by some selected countries for early childhood care and education development.

ECCE in National Five Years Plan

India, in the post-independence period, has developed a plethora of policies, schemes, and plans of actions for children. A brief analysis of these will be useful, insofar as they impinge on early childhood care and education.

Although the national strategic planning process was started in 1952, programmes for childcare did not appear in the first three successive Five Years Plans (1951-66). The Fourth Plan (1969-74), for the first time, laid focus on accelerating the provision of basic services for children, and provided a platform for the adoption of a National Policy for Children in 1974. Subsequently, child welfare programmers have been incorporated in national planning. The Fifth Plan (1974-79) saw a shift in focus from child welfare to child development and an emphasis on integration and convergence of sectoral social inputs for the well-being of infants, children, and pregnant and lactating women.[7] This was reflected in the launch of Integrated Child Development Services (ICDS) in 1975, which aimed to enhance the holistic development of the child through the involvement of a community based volunteer called an Anganwadi worker. The Sixth Five Year Plan (1980-85) provided for the expansion of ICDS projects and implementation of Universalisation of Elementary Education (UEE). The Seventh Five Year Plan (1985-90) set out a strategy for early childhood survival and development. The Eighth Five Year Plan (1992-97) viewed children as the nation's future human resource and investment in child development services as an investment in the country's future. The Ninth Five Year Plan (1997-2002) laid emphasis on three major areas of child development – namely, health, nutrition and education. The Tenth Five Year Plan (2002-07) viewed "Development of Children" not only as the most desirable social investment for the country's future, but as the right of every child to achieve his/her full development potential. The 10th Five Year Plan was committed to adopt a Rights-based approach to the development of children. The 11th Five Year Plan (2007-2012) is the most significant, for two reasons.

First, to a great extent, the objectives of the plan are intertwined with the principles of the CRC. The Plan strives to create a protective environment, which will ensure every child's right to survival, participation, protection, and development.[8]

Secondly, the plan reflects the 86th Constitutional Amendment Act, which altered the statutory basis for elementary education and early childhood care and education. The plan recognizes the UEE and proposes that services should reach all categories of children including children with disabilities, who are discriminated against the education system. As far childcare is concerned, the 11th Five Year Plan adopts the following strategies to ensure child rights in childhood:

- Developing specific interventions to address malnutrition, neo-natal, and infant mortality.
- Recognizing the crèches and day care are important for child development, and empowerment of women, and retention of girls in schools.
- Recognizing that most children are best cared for in their families, policy should strengthen family capabilities to care and protect the child. There must be institutional care for those children who need it.

As regards to ECE, the 11th Five Year Plan recognizes that childcare programmes, crèche programmes, and pre-school interventions are critical. As far as pre-school education is concerned, around 44 per cent of pre-school aged children do not have access to the pre-school activities provided under ICDS; nor do they access private initiatives. The plan acknowledges a large gap between the number of pre-school children and available pre-school services. ECCE facilities in urban areas are insufficient where as ICDS coverage in urban slums is limited.

In order to ensure universalisation of ICDS with quality service, the 11th Five Year Plan proposed to restructure the ICDS scheme so that it focuses on child nutrition, health care, immunization, and early childhood education. ICDS is to be restructured in a 'mission mode' with an integrated structure linking federal and state level. At district level, committees comprising District Collector, District Health Officer, Women Panchayat Members, and mothers group will be set up to decide the targets for ICDS. A Village Committee comprising mothers and representatives of mothers groups, AWW, ANM, ASHA, and Women Panchayats Members will be constituted to look at the issues like the appointment of AWW, AWH, the content of SNP, and procurement. In order to tackle malnutrition among the under 3-year olds, the plan introduces an Intensive Malnutrition Control Programme within the ICDS Scheme. Under this, 6-8 hours crèche service shall be provided to the under-3 in the most nutritionally impoverished districts of the country. Regarding the PSE for children in the 3-6 years age group, approach paper of 11th Five Year Plan had suggested to integrate the pre-school education component under SSA in order to streamline the functioning of the ICDS centers. The 11th Five Year Plan proposes increased allocation of resources not only to expand the coverage of services but also to ensure the availability of adequate infrastructure. All ICDS centers should have a kitchen, a baby-friendly toilet, clean drinking water facilities, and adequate space for children to play.

National Policy for Education

The Constitution of India is the basic document and source of all policy documents of the State, including those dealing with education. The provisions of the constitution relevant to education are;

- Provision of free and compulsory education to all children in the ages of 6-14 years.
- Provision of early childhood care and education to all children below the age of 6 years.
- Education in general, save higher and technical education, is the concurrent responsibility of Union and States.

- Local authorities (Panchayats and Municipalities) have role in school, non- formal education, as per respective state's legislation.

There are two comprehensive policy statements on education in India, in 1968 and 1986.The National Policy of 1968 on Education was the result of the renewed priority assigned to Government of India during the tenure of the then Prime Minister, Rajiv Gandhi. A Committee constituted in 1990 under the chairmanship of Acharya Rammurti reviewed the 1986 policy. On the basis of the recommendations of the committee, certain provisions of 1986 policy were modified in 1992.

There was no direct reference to early childhood care and education or pre-school education in National Policy on Education, 1968. However, the policy committed the government to work on in a bid to provide free and compulsory education for all children, as set out in Article-45 of the Constitution.

The policy also prescribed common schooling system in order to promote social cohesion and national integration. The NPE, 1986 (modified in 1992) emphasized on the need to invest in the development of young children, particularly children from the families of first generation learners. Recognizing the need for the holistic development of children in terms of nutrition, health, and social, mental, physical, moral and emotional development, NPE accorded the highest priority to early childhood care and education. NPE insisted that ECCE should be integrated with ICDS Programmes and with Day-care centers. ECCE Programmes should be child centered and formal methods of learning should be discouraged at this stage. NPE insisted for full integration of childcare and pre-primary education as a feeder and strengthening factor for primary education and for human resource development.

National Plan of Action for Children, 2005

To pave the way for universal early childhood care and education, the NPA has four goals ;

- Universal early childhood services to support children's physical, social, emotional and cognitive development.
- Care and protection and development opportunities to be available to all children below 3 years.
- Pre-school learning, integrated with care and development to be available to all children aged 3-6 years.
- Day care and crèche facilities to be available to parents in rural and urban areas.

Right of Children to Free and Compulsory Education (RTE) Act, 2009

In terms of international human rights instruments, ECCE is considered an integral part of the child's right to education. Unfortunately this was not the approach of 86th Constitutional Amendment Act. The RTE Act does not take a comprehensive approach to early childhood care and education. Even though Section-11 of the Act says about early childhood care and education, this does not mandate the state to make provision for delivering the service.

India officially is the world's second most populous country and most populous democracy in the world is governed on the principles of the Rule of Law, established in the Constitution of India. The Constitution, which came into force on 26 January 1950, is the largest and most exhaustive constitution of any sovereign country. It has accommodated and assimilated some provisions from the Constitution of United States of America (Federal System, Fundamental Rights), United Kingdom (Parliamentary Democracy), Germany (Weimer Constitution), the Republic of Ireland (Directive Principles of State Policy), Russia (Fundamental Duties), and Canada (Distribution of Powers between Center and States).

The Union of India consists of 29 States and 7 Union Territories. India has a federal system with a parliamentary form of democracy. The Constitution of India is the supreme law of the land and all the organs of the government derive their powers from it. The divisions of powers are made between the Union and States on the basis of Union List, State List and Concurrent List. The Union Legislature called Parliament is bi-cameral consist of Council of States (Rajya Sabha) and House of People (Lok Sabha).

Internationally, India is held in very high regard. As a sovereign nation state, India became a member of United Nations General Assembly and signatory state to Universal Declaration of Human Rights (UDHR) 1948 as well as to various international declarations. India has ratified the United Nations' Convention on the Rights of the Child; (UNCRC) 1989 on 11 December 1992. Now it becomes a major global economic player. The country has economic alliances with all the developed and major developing countries of the world. India is one of the five developing countries (the others are Brazil, China, Mexico, and South Africa) which are the members of Group of Eight Countries (G-8 Countries-France, USA, UK, Russia, Germany, Japan, Italy, Canada). India is also member of the G-20 countries comprising 19 countries (Argentina, Australia, Brazil, Canada, France, Germany, India, Indonesia, Italy, Japan, Mexico, Russia, Saudi Arabia, South Africa, South Korea, Turkey, United Kingdom, and USA) and European Union. India continues to remain the major power within the South Asia Association for Regional Cooperation (SAARC) Countries-comprising Bangladesh, Bhutan, India, Maldives, Nepal, Pakistan, and Sri Lanka.

It has witnessed many developments since its independence from the British administration on August 15, 1947. Internationally, India is now recognized as major power with advanced capabilities in science, and technology. India became a nuclear power in 1974 and is now the sixth nuclear power in the world. It has also made substantial progress in terms of economic development also. India has one of the fastest growing economies and is now considered as one of the emerging super powers. With an estimated value of US $ 1.237 trillion, its economy is the 12th largest in the world. However, from development perspective, the pace of progress is far from convincing. The Human Development

Index[9] (HDI) for India is 0.609: In terms of Life Expectancy at Birth, India is ranked 127. India stands in the rank of 118 in Adult Literacy Rate, and 134 in Combined Primary, Secondary, and Tertiary GER. Despite impressive economic growth in recent years, poverty reduction remains slow. As per HDI Report-2008, India has the largest concentration of poor people in the World and Human Poverty Index for the country is 28.5 per cent with the rank of 87. The country has a higher rate of malnutrition among the children under the age of five years than any other country.

India is a country characterized by unity in diversity. India is secular despite the fact it is a multi-culture, multi-language and multi-religion country and is the largest democracy in the world. Despite impressive economic growth, Purchasing Power Parity (PPP) is low. This is a country where large proportions of the population are impoverished and hardly afford to get basic civic amenities. India's characteristics are highly distinctive. Conversely, the United States of America is democratic, but less populated and highly developed. China is populous, but not democratic on the other hand Sri Lanka is poor and democratic, but small.

Each and every country of the world is unique in its own way- be it in geographic location, demographic pattern, economic development, culture, and form of government. It is hard to identify countries, which would offer appropriate comparisons with India in regard to ECCE policies and outcomes. We have however identified several countries that have specific ECCE policies/laws or where priority is given to early childhood care and education for securing the goal of Education for All. The countries which are selected are: Canada, Australia, Ireland, USA, UK, Albania, Brazil, Turkey, Thailand, China, Philippines, Sri Lanka, Indonesia, Mongolia, Vietnam, Guatemala, Egypt, Nigeria and Senegal.

This section examines the approaches taken by these countries to the key issues such as childcare, early childhood education, and other pre-school services. As countries have different policies and provisions, this section also examines service delivery methods.

Comparative Data on Human Development: India & Selected Countries

Country	HDI Value/ Country's HDI Rank	Life Expectancy at Birth/ Country's Rank	Adult Literacy Rate/ Country's Rank	Combined (Primary, Secondary, Tertiary) GER	GDP Per Capita (PPP) in US % / Country's Rank	Human Poverty Index / Country's Rank	Under-5 Children Underweight in % / Country's Rank
1	2	3	4	5	6	7	8
Canada	0.966 R- 4	80.6 R- 11	***	99.3 R- 7	35812 R- 18	***	***
Australia	0.970 R-2	81.4 R- 5	***	114.2 R- 1	34923 R- 22	***	***
Ireland	0.965 R- 5	79.7 R- 18	***	97.6 R- 10	44613 R- 10	***	***
United States of America	0.950 R- 13	79.1 R- 26	***	92.4 R- 21	45592 R- 9	***	***

contd...

1	2	3	4	5	6	7	8
United Kingdom	0.947 R- 21	79.3 R- 24	***	89.2 R- 34	35130 R- 20	***	***
Brazil	0.813 R- 75	72.2 R- 81	90.0 R- 71	87.2 R- 40	9567 R- 79	8.6 R- 43	6 R- 37
China	0.772 R- 92	72.9 R- 72	93.3 R- 56	68.7 R- 112	5383 R-102	7.7 R- 36	7 R- 46
Philippines	0.751 R- 105	71.6 R- 90	93.4 R- 54	79.6 R- 58	3046 R- 124	12.4 R- 54	28 R- 108
Sri Lanka	0.759 R- 102	74.0 R- 59	90.8 R-66	68.7 R- 113	4243 R-116	16.8 R- 68	29 R- 113
Indonesia	0.734 R- 111	70.5 R- 99	92.0 R- 61	68.2 R- 115	3712 R-121	17.0 R- 69	28 R- 109

contd...

1	2	3	4	5	6	7	8
Egypt	0.703 R- 123	69.9 R- 102	66.4 R- 119	76.4 R- 79	5349 R- 103	23.4 R- 8.2	6 R- 40
India	0.612 R- 134	63.4 R- 128	66.0 R- 120	61.0 R- 134	2753 R- 126	28.0 R- 88	46 R- 137
Nigeria	0.511 R- 158	47.7 R- 167	72.0 R- 112	53.0 R- 150	1969 R- 141	36.2 R- 114	29 R- 111
Senegal	0.464 R-166	66.2 R- 116	97.3 R- 33	79.2 R- 59	3236 R- 125	12.7 R- 58	6 R- 43

ECCC IN CANADA

Canada as an American country is a federation comprises ten provinces and 3 territories. The political system is characterized by the parliamentary democracy with a constitutional monarchy. With an estimated population of more than 33.4 million.

Progress Towards EFA Goal - 1 in terms of GER in Pre-Primary Education : A Comparative Assesment

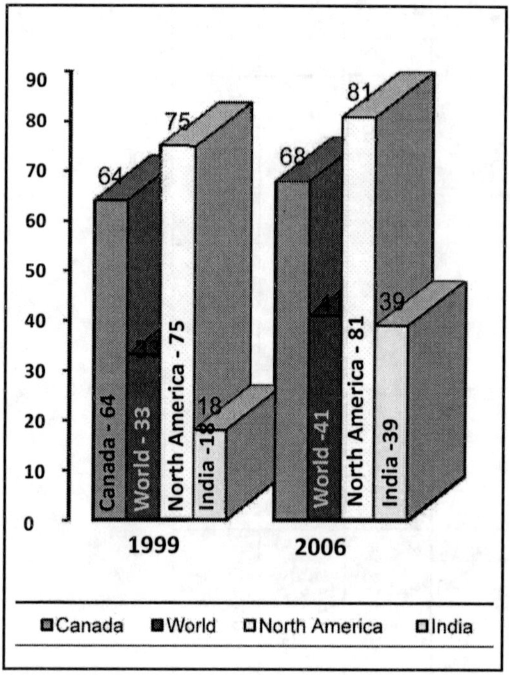

Canada is the world's 36th populous country and renowned for its well-developed education system and one of the best education developed countries of the World. According to the Human Development Report 2009 of UNDP, the HDI for Canada is 0.966, which puts the country in 4th rank among 182 countries. Canada is one of the 38 Very High Human Development Countries of the World. As per the World Bank Assessment, Canada is the 11th largest economies in terms of GDP.]

In Canada, the term Early Childhood Education and Care (ECEC) is commonly used instead of ECCE. There is no national policy or national approach to ECEC or national ECEC legislation[10]. In Canada, education and childcare are regulated in quite different ways. Education including kindergarten is regulated through the public funded/public operated system. Childcare is regulated by private enterprises. The Canadian federal government has no direct responsibility for ECEC. Almost of all ECEC services are under the jurisdiction of the provinces/territories. Each province/ territory has separate programmes and its own approach towards pre-school education, which is delivered in the form of kindergarten.

ECCE IN AUSTRALIA

Australia, officially referred as Commonwealth of Australia, is a country of Southern Hemispheres. Australia is a Federal State having a Parliamentary form of democracy. With a population of around 29 million Australia is the World's 52nd most populous country. According to the Human Development Report of UNDP, the HDI for Australia is 0.970 that gives the country 2nd place among 182 countries. Australia is one of the 38 Very High Human Development Countries of the World. As per the World Bank Assessment in Australia is the 14th largest economy in terms of GDP.

In Australia, Early Childhood Education and Care (ECEC) services are provided to children below school age; i.e. below 6. ECEC services are provided in different formats including Family Day Care, Home Based Care, Long Day Care Centers, Multi Functional Aboriginal Children Services, Mobile Children's Services, Occasional Care Centers.[11] In Australia, school education is universally available for students of compulsory school age. Schooling is delivered through government and non-government providers. Pre-school education in the form of kindergarten or pre-primary is usually provided in the school premises. Commonwealth, State, and Territory governments have jointly

Progress Towards EFA Goal-1 in terms of Pre-Primary Education in GER (in %) in 2006: A Comparative Perspective

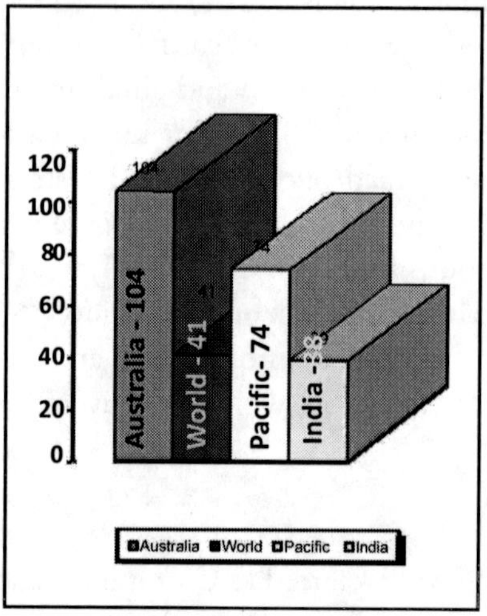

developed a National Minimum Standard, which is being followed for delivering the ECEC services. However, these standards do not have legal enforceability.

ECCE IN IRELAND

Ireland, known as the Irish Republic, is a country of north Western Europe. The country is governed by a Constitution, which came into force on 29 December 1937. Ireland is a republic with a parliamentary system of government. According Human Development Report of UNDP, the HDI for Ireland is 0.960, which puts it in the rank of 5th among 182 countries of the world. Ireland is bracketed among 38 very high human development countries of the world. As per World Bank-2008 list, Ireland is ranked 31 in terms of economic development, i.e. GDP in millions of US dollars. Since the 1990s, early childhood care and education has been the subject of major policy development and statutory provision in Ireland.[12] The Child Care Act, 1991 was the first legislation that required the State to regulate pre-school services and for which Child Care (Pre-School Services) Regulations, 1996 and Child Care (Pre-School Services) (Amendment) Regulations, 1997 were put in place. Children from birth to age of 6 are entitled to receive ECCE.[13] In 2002, a Center for Early Childhood Development and Education (CECDE) was established to co-ordinate, develop and enhance early childhood development and education with special attention to disadvantaged and special needs groups. The principal objective of the CEDEC is to develop a quality framework for early childhood education.

A conceptual framework has been formulated that describes how children below 6 years of age develop and learn. The framework is used as the basis for developing national quality standards in the areas of curriculum/methodology, equipment/ materials, staff/qualifications, and parental involvement. The Framework is designed on the following principles;

- The framework is *eclectic* in orientation and examines critically a variety of theories and documented evidence to explore early childhood (birth to six years) development and learning. It adopts a *holistic* approach to children's development and learning, emphasizing the interplay between the physical, psychological (cognitive, emotional, moral, spiritual) and social aspects.
- It understands children's development and learning in an *ecological* context, considering the micro and macro elements of environmental influence.
- The framework looks at children's achievements in light of their potential and examines their development of a sense of mastery, emphasizing their successes as well as their challenges. It views children as actively engaged in co-constructing their own and other's experiences. Children interact and learn from birth and probably even before. Their active learning does not begin with formal schooling.
- The Framework adopts both right and need based perspectives in line with the UN Convention of the Rights of the Child, 1989 and Irish National Children's Strategy, 2000,
- It emphasizes protective and risk factors, exploring their influence on children's development and learning.

- It examines the historical and contemporary influences of practice, policy and research on children's development and learning in Ireland.

ECCE IN UNITED STATES OF AMERICA

United States of America is the country of North America. USA is a federal state with presidential form of government. With an estimated of 301.13 million population, USA is third largest populous country of the world. According to Human Development Report-2009 of UNDP, the HDI for USA is 0.956 that puts the country in 13th rank. USA is categorized among 38 very high human development countries. As estimated in the World Bank Report-2008, USA is the top ranked economically developed country in terms of GDP.

In USA, there is no national coordinated policy framework for delivering early childhood education and care service to young children. None of the 50 states of USA has established a coherent policy approach concerning early services for children below the compulsory school age. The Public School System is the state-funded kindergarten that is being operated under auspices of education authorities. State sponsored activities include: direct delivery of ECEC services, direct and indirect financial subsidies to private providers of education and care and Financial incentives to parents. The public education system in US is operated by the state and local governments and regulated by the US Department of Education. Compulsory school age is determined by the individual state. Early childhood education (kindergarten) is not mandatory for entering into primary education. Eleven states and the District of Columbia require children to attend kindergarten. The other 39 states require school authorities to provide kindergarten, but it is the discretion of the parents whether or not to enroll their children in kindergarten.[14]

ECCE IN UNITED KINGDOM

The United Kingdom is a country of Continental Europe. The UK has a Constitutional Monarchy with a parliamentary system of government. According Human Development Report-2009 of UNDP, the HDI for United Kingdom is 0.947, which puts it in the rank of 21 among 182 countries of the world. United Kingdom is one of 38 very high human development countries of the world. As per World Bank-2008 list, United Kingdom is world's sixth largest economy in terms of GDP in millions of US dollars.

The UK comprises England, Northern Ireland, Wales and Scotland – each of them have developed slightly different systems for ECEC. Scotland and Wales have devolved responsibility for ECCE and their own legislative competence. At a strategic level, however, this is a large measure of consensus and policy convergence across the UK. The philosophy of the 19th century industrialist and philanthropist Robert Owen had great influence on the development of ECEC policy in UK. Owen was not only a pioneer of infant and nursery movement in UK, but also recognized the need to support families. A well supported family would be more productive and economically useful. The idea of Owen was supported by Scarr (1998), who values the relevance of ECCE in three dimensions.[15] First, it aims to support maternal employment; secondly, it aims to enhance children's development; and thirdly, it aims to intervene with the economically disadvantaged and ethnic minority children to socialize them into mainstream. Later on, the principles of Pestalozzi, Froebel, Steiner and Montessori were influential in the design and delivery of ECEC in UK, though access to services remained uneven and limited, and policy remained uncoordinated, until the 20th century. Although the ECEC was very much diversified and fragmented over a long period of time, the major service providers of ECEC in UK were State, Voluntary Organizations and Private Sectors. Till late 1990s, State's responsibilities for providing ECEC services were few and far between. A milestone in terms of policy development came with the Plowden Report (1964), on primary and nursery education. This stated that nursery provision should not be made available to women who simply wanted to go out to work but should be reserved for those who were most in need of interventionist support. The report also recommended that provision of nursery should be part time rather than full time because nursery provision was fundamentally different from school and its distinctive character – play-based learning - should be preserved. In 1972, ECCE finally secured the attention of the government. The government believes that in the first instance it is the responsibility of parents to make arrangements, including financial arrangements, for the day care of pre-school children".

Voluntary and private ECCE provision remained patchy till the late 1950s but the situation had changed rapidly in 1960's and 70's as more and more women moved into the work place. In the private sector, the expansion of day nurseries was very rapid in the 1980's, increasing by 203 per cent over period 1985-1991. Also in this period, a strong voluntary movement of parent-led playgroups emerged, focusing on part-day support for working parents and a caring and stimulating environment for pre-school children.

ECCE IN BRAZIL

Brazil, officially called as Federative Republic of Brazil, is a country of South America. This is a Democratic Republic with Presidential System of Government. With an estimated population of 190 million, Brazil is 5th largest populous country of the World. According Human Development Report-2009 of UNDP, the HDI for Brazil is 0.813, which place the country a rank of 75 among 182 countries. Brazil is bracketed among 45 High Human Development Countries of the world. As per World Bank-2008 List, Brazil is the 8th largest economy of the world in terms of GDP measured in US dollars.

Even though Pre-School Education/Early Childhood Education is not compulsory, it is being offered through two types of institutions on the basis of the age of the child— day-care centers or equivalent institutions for children up to the age of 3 (nursery education); and pre-primary schools for children aged 4-6 years. Pre-School Programmes are basically run by the Municipalities. As per the Municipal Law, it is mandatory for the Municipality to offer free early childhood and primary education and regulate the provision of early childhood education in private crèches and pre-school institutions.

Progress Towards EFA Goal - 1 in terms of GER in Pre-Primary Education : A Comparative Assesment

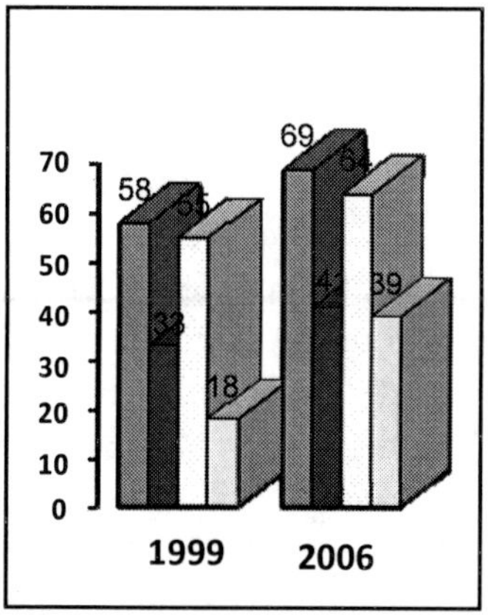

The ECCE Programmes have been governed under the National Plan of Education; 2001.There is also National Education Policy which ensures Pre-School education for all children and early childhood development facilities for the disadvantaged children. The National Child Education Department of the Ministry of Education is responsible for the implementation of ECCE programmes in the Country.[16] The ECCE service providers include Public Agency, Private Partners, and Community Care Givers.

ECCE is understood as pre-school education programme[17] in order to support the mental, emotional, social and psycho motor development of children aged 0-72 months. This programme takes into account the developmental needs of three age groups: 0-36 months (day nurseries), 36-60 months (kindergartens), and 60-72 months (pre-school classes).

Pre-school education is optional and it is given in kindergartens, preparatory classrooms, application classrooms, day nurseries, nursery schools, day-care homes, and childcare homes. A Directorate for Pre-School Education was established in 1992. The Ministry of National Education has overall responsibility for supervision and co-ordination of pre-school education programmes.

ECCE IN THAILAND

Thailand, officially known as the Kingdom of Thailand, is a country of Southeast Asia. It has a Constitutional Monarchy with an estimated population of 65 million; Thailand is the 19th largest country of the world in terms of population. According Human Development Report-2009 of UNDP, the HDI for Thailand is 0.783, which puts it in the rank of 87 among 182 countries of the world. This is one among 75 medium human development countries of the world. As per World Bank-2008 list, Thailand is stood at 35 ranks in terms of GDP in millions of US dollars.

Thailand has a child development plan and a long-term strategy for childhood and youth education from 1979. However, the government decided to develop distinct and focused plan on ECCE in order to address the fundamental needs.[18] In 1999, the National Education Commission with the concurrence of Ministry of Education had made a critical assessment of the status of early childhood care and development from which Thailand's National Education Law (NEL), 1999 was devised. The NEL provided a National Policy Framework for Educational Reform that devises a holistic approach for early childhood care and development. A House Committee constituted to review the National Education Bill had made the following recommendations:

> "Early Childhood Care and Education at present, in terms of the under-fives age group, has not been included in basic education. However, the education provided during this period in life is most crucial, as it forms the basis for subsequent learning and development. The government should therefore

assume a direct or participatory role and provide encouragement and support for individuals, families, community and local administration organizations, private persons, private and professional organizations, religious institutions, enterprises and other social institutions to take part in early childhood development. Such development, of a comparable quality and standard, should be equally provided."

The NEL put emphasis on "reforming the learning process and structure of education by increasing alternatives for educational management and curriculum development, including the provision of quality assurance and opportunities for children to have access to free education for at least 12 years." The law recognized the period of early childhood as a crucial period of brain development and education provided at this level should be for child's development. National ECCE policy has been directed for the following:

- To establish a system of learning networks;
- To provide and promote prenatal care, child-rearing practices and education necessary for child development;
- To prepare every child for entry to primary school;
- To improve curriculum content and teaching-learning processes at all levels and in all types of education;
- To enhance the capability of students and the population in using the Thai language:
- To promote and support the participation of families, local communities, social institutions and mass media in the educational process.

ECCE programmes and policies are being supervised at different levels of ministry in accordance with the principles and guidelines of National Scheme of Education. The Ministry of Education is responsible for developing the curriculum for pre-primary education of 3-5 years aged children. The Office of National Primary Education Commission (ONPEC) under the Office of the Prime Minister has developed and now promotes

"Childcare Standards for the 0-3 Age Group", which consists of four sets of standards pertaining to: (1) qualifications, attributes and responsibilities of childcare providers; (2) nurseries; (3) training institutions for childcare providers, both public and private; and (4) prescribed training courses for childcare providers.

ECCE IN CHINA

China, officially known as People's Republic of China, is a country in East Asia. It is the most populous country in the World with around 1.3 billion people that approximately accounts one-fifth of the World's population. China is a Socialist Republic Country ruled by the Communist Party of China. According to Human Development Report-2009 of UNDP, the HDI for China is 0.772, which gives the country a rank of 92 among 182 countries. China has been categorized among 75 medium human development countries. As per World Bank estimation of 2008, China is third largest economy measured in terms of GDP.

Early childhood education in the People's Republic of China has been inextricably influenced by the changes and progress of politics and economy in Chinese society. As the economic-political scene has undergone a dramatic and tortuous development over the past four decades, the development of China's early childhood education services has experienced a parallel progression.[19]

The educational philosophy of western countries and the missionary activities of imperialist powers strongly influenced China to include pre-school education within the Country's education framework. China has developed a countrywide ECCE policy[20] for nurseries (0-3 years), kindergartens (3-6 years), pre-primary classes (5-6 years) and variety of other forms of child and parent education. The 'Regulations on Work of Kindergartens (1989)', 'Regulations on the Management of Kindergartens (1989)', "Guidelines for the Evaluation of the Work of Pre-Primary Classes (1998)', 'Education Guidelines for Kindergartens (2001), constitute a set of working documents and guidelines for management of early childhood education.[21] In 2003, Early Childhood Care and

Education Reform and Development was enacted to achieve a goal of enrolment rate in pre-school education by 55 per cent by the year 2007. The overall responsibility of ECCE administration is rested with the Ministry of Education with corresponding provincial, municipal, and regional bureaus. The Ministry of Health, Ministry of Planning, Ministry of Labour & Personnel have also entrusted with specific responsibilities in accordance with their work mandate.

There is consensus internationally–ECCE will place children at a better start for primary education and give them a better chance for achievements later in life–in China the importance of ECCE has not caught the full attention of society. This lack of awareness and the uncertainty of parents of the influence of ECCE on the school readiness of their children lead many parents to place ECE far from the top of the education priority list.

ECCE IN PHILIPPINES

Philippines is officially known as the Republic of the Philippines, is a country of Southeast Asia. This is a Unitary State with Presidential System of Government, with an estimated population of 92 million. Philippines is the 12th most populous country of the world. According Human Development Report-2009 of UNDP, the HDI for Philippines is 0.751, which puts it in the rank of 105 among 182 Countries of the World. Philippines is one of the 75 medium human development countries of the World. As per World Bank-2008 list, Philippines is ranked 47 in terms of economic development, i.e. GDP in millions of US dollars.

The Early Childhood Care and Development (ECCD) Law, 2000 recognizes the importance of early childhood and its special needs. It affirms parents as primary caregivers and the child's first teachers, and provides for parent effectiveness seminars and nutrition counseling for pregnant and lactating mothers.[22] The National Coordinating Council for the Welfare of Children establishes;

(a) guidelines, standards, and culturally relevant practices for ECCD programs;

Progress Towards EFA Goal - 1 in terms of GER in Pre-Primary Education : A Comparative Assesment

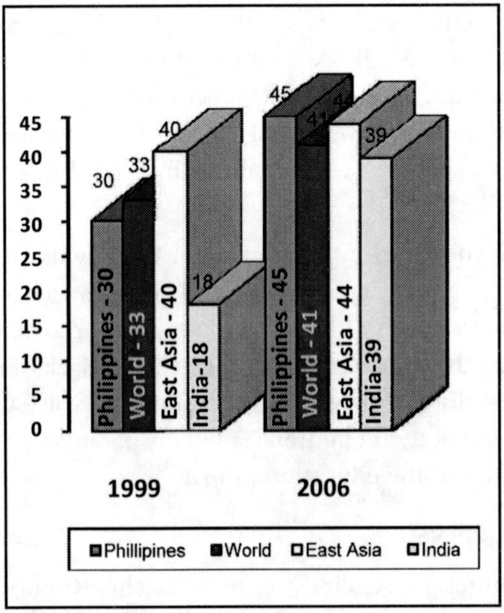

(b) develops a national system for the recruitment, training, and accrediting of caregivers;

(c) monitors the delivery of ECCD services and the impact on beneficiaries;

(d) provides additional resources to poor and disadvantaged communities in order to increase the supply of ECCD programs; and

(e) encourages the development of private sector initiatives.

At the national level, the Department of Social Welfare and Development (DSWD) is the agency responsible for overall policy and programme development, setting and promoting guidelines and standards, providing technical assistance to the local government units through the regional field offices, monitoring and evaluation. At the provincial level, the responsibility for monitoring and supervision has been allocated to the ECCD Coordinating Councils.

The National ECCD programmes focus on:

- Improving infant and child survival rates through expanded child health programs;
- Enhancing the roles of parents and caregivers through parent effectiveness seminars and counseling;
- Enhancing the cognitive, physical, social and emotional development of young children through the establishment of additional child care centers under the Department of Social Welfare;
- Smooth transition from at-home care to pre or primary schools through a two-month bridging program for entrants to primary school;
- Creating a system for early intervention and prevention of developmental problems and disabilities.

ECCE IN SRI LANKA

Sri Lanka, officially referred as Republic of Sri Lanka, is a country in South Asia. It is a democratic, socialistic Republic with unitary political system. Sri Lanka is the 53rd most populous country in the World. According to the Human Development Report-2009 of UNDP, the HDI for Sri Lanka is 0.759 that places the country in 102 rank among 182 countries. Sri Lanka is one among the 75 medium human development countries of the world. As estimated in the World Bank Report-2008, Sri Lanka is placed in a rank of 74 in terms of GDP.

In the Sri Lankan policy context, early childhood is defined as the period 0-5 years. In policy papers, the term ECCD has mostly been used instead of ECCE. There has been a well-organized ECCE management and service delivery structure in Sri Lanka. The Ministry of Education has incorporated ECCE as an important subject under the General Education Reforms of 1997.The action plan unveiled in the Education Reforms called for –

(i) Strengthening the Children Secretariat and Non-Formal Education branch for implementation of planned ECE;

(ii) Designing awareness programme to raise mothers' understanding of child development;

(iii) Making legislative provisions for regulation of pre-school; and

(iv) Setting up a Department of ECCD and Child Study Center. On EFA Goal-1, a National Policy on ECCD was formulated by the Ministry of Women's Empowerment and Social Welfare in 2004. The National Plan of Action-2004, emerging from the National Policy on ECCD, promised to expand and improve early childhood care and development services in order to (i) increase participation of 3-5 years aged children in pre-school education; (ii) improve the quality of pre-school education and train all pre-school teachers; (iii) create awareness on the needs of pre-school education for children among parents and stakeholders. A Department of Early Childhood and Primary Education (DECPE) and a Child Study Center (CSC) have been established at the Open University of Sri Lanka. DECPE carries out the task of providing opportunities for ECCD Field Personnel to obtain professional qualifications.[23]

ECCE in SPAIN

The 2006 Act on Education establishes Pre-Primary Education, an educational stage in its own right which is non-compulsory, as the first stage of the education system. It is organised into two cycles of three years each: the first one, up to 3 years of age, and the second one, from 3 to 6 years of age. The Autonomous Communities regulate the objectives, contents, evaluation, organisation as well as the requirements schools have to meet in the first cycle of the stage. In the second cycle, however, all these aspects are regulated by the State and the Autonomous Communities complete them for their respective regions.

Aims and General Objectives

The aim of pre-primary education is to contribute to the physical, emotional, social and intellectual development of children in close cooperation with families. The two cycles of the stage should progressively pay attention to emotional development, body movement and control, communication and verbal expression, basic guidelines of coexistence and social relations, as well as discovery of the physical and social characteristics of the environment. The development of a positive and balanced image of themselves and the acquisition of personal autonomy should also be encouraged.

In accordance with the Act on Education and the Royal Decree establishing the core curricula for the second cycle of Pre-Primary Education, the general objectives of this stage are the following:

- Know their own and others' bodies, its capacities, and learn to respect differences.
- Observe and explore their family, natural and social environment.
- Acquire progressive autonomy in their regular activities.
- Develop their emotional abilities.
- Socialise with others and progressively acquire the basic guidelines of coexistence and social relations, as well as practice the peaceful resolution of conflicts.
- Develop communicative skills in different languages and types of expression.
- Begin developing logical-mathematical abilities, reading and writing, as well as movement, gesture and rhythm.

The Autonomous Communities, in the exercise of their educational powers, complete the general objectives of the stage.

Schools Providing Pre-Primary Education

Pre-primary education is offered in public or private schools, which may provide the first cycle of the stage, the second or both. Public schools offering Pre-primary education are called Pre-primary schools and those also providing primary education are known as pre-primary and primary schools. Almost every institution which provides pre-primary education is dependent upon the education authorities. In some Autonomous Communities, there are schools for children aged 0 to 3 years which depend upon the social area. In 2011-12, 8638 schools offered the first cycle of pre-primary education throughout the State (4073 were public and 4565 private). Of the 14343 schools which provided the second cycle, 10685 were public, 3069 were publicly-funded private schools and 589 were private. The number of schools varies significantly from one Autonomous Community to another.

Educational Policy

The priorities of Spain's educational policy regarding pre-primary education focus on the improvement of quality and access to education during the first years of life. The Act on Education envisages a free second cycle of pre-primary education, and urges the education authorities to progressively provide enough school places for the first cycle through agreements with the local corporations, other authorities or non-profit private institutions. Therefore, the main lines of action are:

- Continue increasing the number of public school places for children less than 3 years of age.
- Offer enough school places in public schools and establish a system of subsidy arrangements in order to ensure a free second cycle.
- Adapt the schools offering this stage to the minimum requirements established by the Education Authorities, such as facilities or pupil/teacher ratio.

ECCE in Switzerland

The Swiss Civil Code (Article-316) and the Federal Ordinance on the Placement of Children in Foster Care and for Adoption (FCAO) lay down the legal framework conditions governing childcare. The FCAO mainly regulates the approval requirements for childcare and the supervision of such services. The cantons are responsible for the specific application of these provisions. They can perform these tasks themselves or delegate them to the communes or third parties. Childcare for children under four years falls within the sphere of family and social policy. In this context the Swiss Conference of Cantonal Ministers of Social Affairs (SODK) assumes a coordinating role for the cantons. The SODK has adopted recommendations on early childhood childcare.

For day-care centres in the sphere of compulsory education including pre-school. The SODK has adopted, together with the Swiss Conference of Cantonal Ministers of Education (EDK), which undertakes key coordination tasks in education for the cantons, a joint declaration on day-care centres for children. Most cantons mention the promotion of childcare in their constitution or in cantonal laws. Only in one canton do parents have the right to have their children offered a public or private place in childcare within a reasonable time.

Pre-school

Pre-school promotes individual development and social learning and prepares children for starting school. It falls within the sphere of education and is covered by education policy. Attendance of state-run pre-school is free. The cantons regulate pre-school in the cantonal education acts. Important tasks which require Intercantonal coordination are undertaken by the EDK. The communes (and less frequently the private sector) operate pre-school establishments

Depending on the canton pre-school attendance may be compulsory (compulsory attendance) or the cantons may require the communes to provide pre-school (compulsory provision).

- Almost 100% of children attend pre-school for at least one year, and around 86% for two years. Depending on the canton children start pre-school once they have reached the age of four or five, or the age of three in the canton of Ticino. At the request of parents children may start pre-school at a later or earlier stage.
- Under the Intercantonal Agreement on Harmonisation of Compulsory Education (HarmoS Agreement), two years of pre-school will become compulsory in those cantons which have

signed the HarmoS Agreement but do not yet offer a compulsory two-year pre-school; children will start once they have reached the age of four (this will be implemented from the start of the 2015-16 school year at the latest). In most cantons which have not signed the HarmoS Agreement, or have not yet started the ratification process, pre-school attendance of at least one year is compulsory. Many of these cantons also offer two years of pre-school.

ECCC IN INDONESIA

Indonesia, officially known as Republic of Indonesia, is a country in Southeast Asia. With a population of 237 million, Indonesia is the World's 4th populous country. This is Unitary State with Presidential form of Government. According to Human Development Report-2009 of UNDP, the HDI for Indonesia is 0.734 that puts it in a rank of 111 among 182 countries. Indonesia is categorized among 75 medium human developed countries. Indonesia is the 15th ranked country in terms of GDP, as per the World Bank estimation in 2008. The issues are derived from 3 years intensive observation and analysis of ECCE on five contributing conditions such as the history and technology of its development: objective conditions and its human resources, socio economic and cultural conditions, current Govt. polices and optimism and beliefs on the investment.[24]

In Indonesia, Early Childhood Care and Education is being offered to children between 0-6 years in five major forms of departmental responsibilities, and institutional delivery. Where care and education are divided, the prime responsibility for PSE lies with the Department of Education.

ECCE In Four Arab Countries

ECCE Services in four Arab countries of Lebanon, Jordan, Sudan and Syria.

This part examines ECCE services in four Arab countries; Jordan, Lebanon, Sudan, and Syria. The services involve several aspects such as the supply of these services, the degree of access, the extent of financing and by whom, and the quality of these services. Equitable access to ECCE programmes can strengthen learning, reduce social inequalities, and support the educational and social needs of families. Most of these programmes are supplied by the private sector. The private sector comprises profit making businesses which are mostly provided in formal, institutional settings and non-profit community-based or NGOs or funded by international NGOs often in non-formal settings. In order to better understand the factors facilitating or hindering the provision and access to ECCE services; it is useful to examine the factors that have impacted the development of early childhood programmes. For a period of history, each of these countries was under Western colonial rule that introduced Western education through its missionaries. For example, the earliest form of pre schools began in the 19th century in countries like Lebanon, Sudan, and Syria.

Asia-Pacific Regional Policy Forum on ECCE

The Asia-Pacific Regional Policy Forum on Early Childhood Care and Education took place in Seoul, Republic of Korea from 10 to 12 September 2013. Under the subtitle "Are children ready to learn? Are schools ready for children?" The Forum focused on improving young children's 'readiness to learn' from both children's and school's perspectives, with special attention to the promotion of equity. With almost 200 high-level representatives from 31 countries in the Asia-Pacific region participating, including 18 education ministers and vice-ministers, the forum bolstered the early childhood development community's commitment to children, underscoring the importance of an inter-sect oral holistic approach. At the end of the Forum, participating delegations presented and discussed follow-up actions to be undertaken in their respective countries as well as mechanisms for future country-to-country cooperation.

From world point of view, it is proved that Early Childhood

Care and Education is an important aspect of all round development of the child. Educationalist, psychologists are also agreed upon this thing that early childhood period is very crucial for the all round development of the individual. It laid down the foundation stone of a child for successful transition from pre-primary to primary level.

References

1. Desmond, C., (2001) 'Time to Reformat', article in Children First Journal, op. cit.
2. https://webgate.ec.europa.eu/fpfis/mwikis/eurydice/index.php/ Spain: Early_Childhood_Education_and_Care.
3. https://webgate.ec.europa.eu/fpfis/mwikis/eurydice/index.php/ Switzeland:Early_Childhood_Education_ and _care.
4. Op. cit., Children First Journal Aug/Sept 2001
5. Sources: ap-ecce-forum@unesco.org
6. Strong Beginnings – Learning to Live publication of SCF (USA) 2001.
7. Torkington, K., (2001), WGECD Policy Project – A Synthesis Report ADEA unpublished Op cit Torkington and Irvine 2002.
8. Torkington, K. and Irvine, M., (2002) 'Guidelines on ECD Policy Issues in Africa' in preparation, ADEA.
9. Torkington, K., and Landers, C., (1995, 2nd edition 1999, '*Enhancing the Skills of Early Childhood Trainers*' UNESCO (Paris) and Bernard van Leer Foundation, Den Haag.
10. Torkington, K. and Landers, C., (1995, 2nd edition 1999, 'Enhancing the Skills of Early Childhood Trainers' UNESCO (Paris) and BVLF, Den Haag.
11. Van de Linde, T., Evers, Y. and Smale, J., (2001) 'Family Support Workshop' in Children First Journal Aug/Sept 2001, Durban, RSA.
12. Wood, A.W. (1990) Presentation at World Conference on Basic Education, Jomtien, Thailand 1990).
13. World Bank (1996) Report of Conference on ECD Atlanta, April 1996.

Notes

1. Convention on the Rights of the Child. The United Nations Convention on the Rights of the Child, November 20, 1989, set an International standard for the ECCE as rights of the child.
2. Education for All: The Dakar Framework for Action World Education Forum Dakar, Senegal, 26-28 April 2000.
3. EFA Global Monitoring Report; 2009, UNESCO.
4. In reference to EFA Global Monitoring Report- 2009, In Argentina, Pre-School attendance from age 3-5 increased performance in language (ii) In Uruguay; pre-school attendance had a positive effect on completed years of schooling, repetition rates and age-grade distortion. In Cambodia, the availability of pre-school facilities increased the probability of successful school completion from 43% to 54%.
5. http://data.worldbank.org/indicator/SE.PRE.ENRR
6. Position Paper National Focus Group on Early Childhood Education, National Council of Educational Research and Training, 2006.
7. National Policy for Children, 1974.
8. http://www.childlineindia.org.in/Child-Rights-in-the-Five-Year-Plans.htm
9. This statistical information is downloaded from website- http:// hdrstatus: undp.org (Since 1990, Human Development Report Office United Nations Development Programme (UNDP) has been publishing HDI in each year. The afore-mentioned ranking is in terms of HDI-2008. The HDI provides a composite measure of the three dimensions of human development: living long and healthy life (measured by life expectancy); being educated (measured by adult literacy, enrolment at the primary, secondary, and tertiary level); and having decent standard of living (measured by the income and Purchasing Power Parity).
10. OECD Thematic Review of ECEC.
11. OECD Thematic Review of ECEC; Australian Background Report; Prepared by the Institute of Early Childhood, Division of ECEC & Education of Macquaire University, Sydney.

12. A Conceptual Framework of Young Children 's Development and Learning in Ireland: The Implications for quality in Early Years Care and Education; A Paper Presented by the Director of CECDE in EECERA Conference, September, 2004.

13. In reference to the Report of the Expert Working Group on Childcare (Department of Justice, Equality and Law Reform, 1999) and the White Paper on Early Childhood Education (Department of Education and Science, 1999).

14. http://en.wikipedia.org/wiki/Category:Early_childhood_education_in_the_United_States

15. www.-oecd--ilibrary.-org/-education/-quality--matters--in--early--childhood--education--and--care--united--kingdom--england--2012_97892641768-67.

16. http://www.bernardvanleer.org/Early_Childhood_in_Brazil_General_overview_and_current_issues

17. Turkey Early Childhood Care and Education Programees: Country Profile Commissioned for the EFA Global Monitoring Report 2007, UNESCO International Bureau of Education (IBE), Geneva, Switzerland.

18. http://www.unicef.org/thailand/education_14938.htm

19. The Past, Present and Future of Chinese Early Childhood Education, Caven S. Mcloughlin, Kent State University, USA.

20. Selected Issues Concerning ECCE in China; Background Paper For EFA Global Monitoring Report- 2007.

21. China ECCE Programmes; Compiled by UNESCO International Bureau Education; Geneva, Switzerland.

22. Philippines Early Childhood Care and Education Programmes UNESCO International Bureau of Education (IBE) Geneva, (Switzerland) 2006.

23. Early Childhood Care and Development in Sri Lanka, by Chitrangani Abhayadeva.

24. Ali Nugraha and Hani Yulindrasari, Indonesia University of Education (UPI), Bandung, Indonesia.

4

Early Childhood Care and Education: Isssues and Challenges

Legal Framework of ECCE and Institutional Facilities

Early childhood years is a very special period in every human beings life cycle. It is the foundation stone of human life to achieve the optimal physical growth and psychological development. Early Childhood Care and Development (ECCD) are very important for the survival, growth and development of the child. The term growth and development shall have a qualitative dimension. It is not only extended to mean physical growth or health but also the emotional, cognitive and social development of the child.

India as the second largest populous country of the world with a population of more than 164.5 million.[1] India accounts for a meager 2.4 per cent of the world surface area and shares 16.7 percent of the world population. India has also second highest child population in the world. Near about 41 per cent of India's total population are children below the age of 18 years. The 0-6 year child population, as per Census-2011, is more than 164.5 million, which is more than 19.9 percent of the country's total population. The total population of pre-school children (0-6 years) as recorded in the census 2011 was more than 8.36 million which constituted 19.5 per cent population.

India is a country of large cultural and linguistic diversity. As many as 533 categories of tribes are residing across the country.

The country is governed by a constitution, which envisages a parliamentary form of government both at the union and state level and having a federal set-up, constitutional governance with joint responsibility of the central government and the state government.

ECCE in Constitutional Framework of India

The concept of ECCE as such was no where coined in the Constitution of India. This is a lateral entry and as of now ECCE is an explicit provision under Article-45 of the constitution the Constitution of India. This does not mean that there was no constitutional inference that reposed obligation of State towards the young children. There are several provisions under the Constitution of India in the Directive Principles of State Policy that have been used to promote ECCE services in the country.[2] The specific provisions under the Directive Principles of State Policy (DPSP) that provide a supportive framework for ECCE in the country.

Article 39(f): The State shall, in particular, direct its policy towards securing that children are given opportunities and facilities to develop in a healthy manner and in conditions of freedom and dignity and that childhood are protected against exploitation. This provision is in the interest of health and strength of young persons and is in keeping with the provisions of the directives in Article 39(e) and (f) of the Constitution where the state, in particular, direct its policy towards securing – (e) that the health and strength of workers, men and women, and the tender age of children are not abused and that citizens are not forced by economic necessity to enter a vocations unsuited to their age or strength; (f) that children are given opportunities and facilities to develop in a healthy manner and in conditions of freedom and dignity and that childhood and youth, are protected against exploitation and against moral and material abandonment.[3]

Article 42: The state shall make provision for securing just and humane conditions of work and maternity relief.

Article 45: Prior to 86th Constitution Amendment Act, 2002, there was a provision that the verbatim of that Article was like this, "the state shall endeavor to provide, within a period of ten years from the commencement of the Constitution, for free and compulsory education for all children until the age of 14 years." The 86th Amendment has revised the erstwhile provision of Article 45 to read: "The state shall endeavor to provide early childhood care and education for all children until they complete the age of 0-6 years of age."

Article 47: The State shall endeavor to raise the level of food, nutrition and the standard of living of its people to improve health.

Issues of ECCE in National Policy Framework

Early Childhood Care and Education involves the multiple components such as health, nutrition, pre-primary education, and childcare services etc. As a result of which, policies have been formulated in various point of time for delivering the services to the young children.

OBJECTIVES OF VARIOUS NATIONAL POLICIES

National Policy for Children, 1974

The National Policy for Children, 1974 has adopted an integrated approach to address the whole child by stating that "It shall be the policy of the State to provide adequate services to the children, both before and after birth and throughout the period of growth. The State progressively increases the scope of such services so that, within a reasonable time, all children in the country enjoy optimum conditions for their balanced development.[4]"

National Policy on Education, 1986

Early Childhood Care and Education views *as* a critical input in the strategy of human resource development, as a support programme for primary education and also as a support service for working women. This policy recognizes the holistic nature of child development, and that ECCE is the crucial foundation for human resource development and cumulative lifelong learning[5] it categorically emphasizes investment in the development of young children, particularly children from sections of the population in which first generation learners predominate. The policy aimed to bring about a full integration of childcare and pre-primary education in order to feed and strengthen primary education.

National Plan of Action, 1992

The plan of action advocated for the expansion of early childhood development activities with special emphasis on appropriate and low cost family and community interventions. It also aimed to reduce the low birth weight babies and malnutrition among the under-5 children.

National Nutrition Policy, 1993

National Nutrition Policy recognizes that the children below 6 years are nutritionally vulnerable and constitute one of the high risk groups, and thus accords highest priority to them through policy articulations and programmatic interventions for especially vulnerable groups. National Nutrition Mission (NNM) has been launched to address this problem.

National Health Policy, 2002

This policy is giving maximum emphasis for the preventive and curative care at the primary health level, and emphasizes convergence, and strategies to care behaviuors in families and communities. The children of 0-6 years comprise a vital segment of the NHP as it aims to reduce IMR to 30, and MMR to 100 by the year 2010. Separate schemes are also proposed to address the health needs of the children of the tribal and other socio-economically undeserved sections.

National Plan of Action for Children, 2005

The Ministry of Women and Child Development (WCD) has prepared the plan of action in order to fulfill the constitutional obligation towards children and the commitment of government in implementing the provisions of the Convention on the Rights of the Child in domestic sphere. As far as Early Childhood Care and Education is concerned, NPA sets the following goal to achieve: The National Plan of Action for Children, 2005 commits itself to ensure all rights to all children up to the age of 18 years.

The Government shall ensure all measures and an enabling environment for survival, growth, development and protection of all children, so that each child can realize his or her inherent potential and grow up to be a healthy and productive citizen.[6] However there are some instinct features of this policy:

1. To universalize early childhood services to ensure children's physical, social, emotional and cognitive development.
2. To ensure that care and protection and development opportunities are available to all children below 3 years.
3. To ensure integrated care and development and pre-school learning opportunities for all children aged 3-6 years.
4. To provide day care and crèche facilities to parents in rural and urban areas.

Provisions Relating to Young Children in India

There are numbers of legislations in India that directly or indirectly have a bearing on the survival, protection, and development of young children. In India, we have broadly three kinds of statutory provisions that concern with the issues of young children.

One kind of statutory provision is concerned with the survival rights of the child, the protection and promotion of child rights. The second kind statues prescribe the service delivery systems in order to ensure child rights.

There are some statues that are not exclusively for children but they provide childcare services in certain work situation. The statue noted below comes under the first category of statutory provisions. Pre-Conception and Pre-Natal Diagnostic Techniques (Prevention of Misuse and Prohibition of Sex Selection) Act, 1994

(Amended in 2003) regulates the use of the techniques in order to prevent the misuse of such techniques for the purpose of pre-natal sex determination leading to female foeticide.

Infants Milk Substitutes, Feeding Bottles, Infant Foods (Regulation of Production, Supply, and Distribution), popularly known as IMS Act, 1992 (Amended in 2003) aims to protect and promote the breast-feeding and to ensure proper use of infant food.[7] The second set of statutory framework is of the following:

> Registration of Births and Deaths Act, 1969 prescribes uniform provision for birth registration in order to maintain accurate countrywide data for national planning.

Juvenile Justice, (JJ) (Care & Protection of Children) Act, 2000 (Amended in 2006) creates service delivery mechanism for the rehabilitation of child in need of care and protection through adoption, foster care, or institutional care. Among the third category of statue, the following legislation comes which have provisions of child care in form of crèche, day care or nursery:

- Factories Act, 1948
- Mines Act, 1950
- Plantation Labour Act, 1951
- Maternity Benefit Act, 1961
- Beedi and Cigar Workers Act, 1966
- Contract Labour Act, 1970
- Building and Other Construction Workers Regulation Act, 1996
- National Rural Employment Guarantee Act, 2006.

Various Issues of ECCE in Country's Five Year Plan

Constitutionally, Child Development and Child Education is the subject of the Concurrent List (List-3 of the Seventh Schedule of the Constitution of India), which implies joint responsibility of the Union Government and State Government in delivering of services. Considering the size of the young child population and constitutional directives, early childhood care and development plan of action might have been prioritized in the Country's Five Year Plans. Unfortunately, childcare and development received a less attention of the policy makers in the first three five year plans. Until the Third Five-Year Plan, ECCE continued to be within the purview of voluntary organizations and private sectors. The diverse socio-economic geographic condition of the country results in diverse need of the children. Keeping in view, the government adopt inclusive approach for the development, protection of the children by addressing specific needs and concern with special emphasis on physical, emotional, cognitive development of the child.[8]

It was in 1966, the Education Commission had recognized the significance of pre-school education and its critical linkages with the enrolment, retention, and learning outcomes at the primary level and also recommended the State to take responsibility for supervision, guidance, and setting up of model schools, training, and research concerning early childhood education. Again in 1968, the Ganga Saran Sinha Committee recognized pre-school education as an instrument for expanding primary school enrolment, reducing dropouts and forming desirable attitudes and habits, especially for children coming from economically and socially backward families. The committee had also recommended for heavy investment on pre-school education. Consequent upon those recommendations, planning strategies for children were evolved and early childhood care and development has been considered as positive determinant for human development.

The Fourth Five Year Plan introduced Family and Child Welfare Scheme for rural areas with the objectives to foster all round development of pre-school child and to strengthen the family so that it could contribute to optimal development of its children.

The Fifth Five Year Plan was instrumental for the adoption of National Policy for Children in 1974 by virtue of which the concept of child development had seen a major shift from *welfare* to *development* approach.

The Fifth Five Year Plan emphasized integration and convergence of segregated services into one component for which Integrated Child Development Services (ICDS) was launched in 1975 on an experimental basis in 33 projects. Until the Eighth Five Year Plan, the care and education pre-school children was restricted within the government sector.

The Ninth Five Year Plan reaffirmed the priority accorded to the development of early childhood services as an investment in *human resource development*. The Tenth Five Year Plan adopts a right-based approach to child development. In order to ensure the development two nationwide major programmes – Reproductive Child Health and Sarva Shiksha Abhiyan- relating to health, nutrition and education were launched

Opportunity for ECCE Service

ECCE service for 0-6 year children is, broadly, being provided at three levels - Private Sector, NGO Sector, and Government Sector. Through private sector initiatives, early childhood care and education service is rendered in different nomenclature, i.e. nurseries, kindergartens, crèche, day care etc. Private sector initiatives are commercial venture and mostly confined in urban and semi-urban areas and for the children of higher and upper-middle class families. There are also facilities for ECCE services in non-government sector. Funded by the international organization, international & national donors, international and national trust, as well as by the government, the Non-Government Organizations, or Voluntary Organizations too have provided ECCE service through their project based intervention.

There is also large number of government-sponsored progarammes and policies directed towards the 0-6 year aged children. Since government has a constitutional obligation of making provision for providing ECCE service to all children below the age six years, this is really pertinent to delineate how far the government has been succeeded in this endeavour and what type of programmes have been put in place.

At the threshold, this is to put that there are three government sponsored programmes - ICDS, SSA, and Crèche- through which ECCE service is being delivered. Among the three, ICDS is the largest programme and provides comprehensive package of services through AWC. In the programmes like District Primary Education Programme (DPEP), and Sarva Siksha Abhiyan (SSA), efforts have been made to open Early Childhood Education Center in non-ICDS covered areas in order to fill the void.

As per government report[9], DPEP has opened 10,000 ECE centers in non-ICDS areas. SSA also has aim to:

(i) Strengthen the pre-school component in ICDS;

(ii) Build advocacy for the importance of early childhood development;

(iii) Organize training programmes for community leaders;

(iv) Provide for intensive planning for ECCE;

(v) Develop materials; and

(vi) Promote convergence between the school system and ECCE. Crèche service is being provided through Rajiv Gandhi National Crèche Scheme for the Children of Working Mothers.

Integrated Child Development Services (ICDS)

ICDS was launched in the year 2nd October, 1975- on the eve of the 106th birth anniversary of Mahatma Gandhi, the father of the nation. ICDS is centrally sponsored schemes of the Ministry of Women & Child Development (WCD) of Government of India. ICDS is the country's most comprehensive and multi-dimensional programme in India which aims at to enhance the holistic development of the child by catering the services through the network of Anganwadi Centers and with the involvement of community based voluntary worker called Anganwadi Worker.

Objectives of ICDS

- To lay foundation for the proper psychological, physical, and social development of the child.

- To improve the nutritional and health status of the children below the age of 6 years.
- To reduce the incidence of mortality, morbidity, malnutrition, and school dropouts.
- To achieve effective coordination of policy and implementation among various departments to promote child development.
- To enhance the capability of the mother to look after the normal health and nutritional needs of the child through proper health and nutritional status.
- In order to achieve the multi-fold objectives, ICDS through the network of Anganwadi Centers, provides a package of services that include, (i) supplementary nutrition, (ii) immunization; (iii) health check-up, (iv) non-formal pre-school education;(v) nutrition & health education, and (vi) referral services.

Operational Setting

ICDS has a line of administrative and organizational structure. The Administrative Unit for the location of an ICDS Project is a Community Development Block in rural areas, Tribal Development Block in the tribal areas, and a group of slums in urban areas. It is a centrally sponsored scheme and the Ministry of Women & Child Development of Government of India designs its policy formulation. The implementation of the schemes lies with the State Government and Department of Women & Child Development of State Governments oversee its implementation. The administrative structure is hierarchical and decentralized. At each stage, key officials are in charge of service delivery responsibilities. The District Social Welfare Officer/DSWO and District Welfare Officer is responsible for overall implementation of the programme in the respective district. Each ICDS Project Block has a Child Development Project Officer (CDPO) for overseeing the programme. At the village level, the AWW is the focal point for delivering the services to the beneficiaries.

Pre-School Education

Under the ICDS scheme, pre-school education is a vital service component for 3-6 year aged children. The subject of 'Pre-School Education' has been allocated to the Ministry of Women and Child Development by the amendment. The ICDS guidelines prescribes pre-school education through non-formal and play way methods by joyful learning. Under the ICDS policy, pre-school education is termed as school preparatory stage for which focus should be on concept formation and language development by organizing activities like pre-conversation, storytelling, vocabulary building. Although States/Union Territories shall have their own choice for developing pre-school kits, the Revised ICDS Guidelines[10] provides a suggestive list for the preparation of the kits:

- Flash cards for story telling
- Model pictures books of animals, fruits, vegetables, parts of the body
- Building blocks
- Suffered toys
- Dolls for role play
- Colours, number, alphabet, matching cards
- Stacking rings/Shape Tower
- Balls
- Threading Boards/Beads & Wires
- Kitchen Set
- Wheel Toys
- Dhapli/small drum
- Simple Puzzels

ICDS Coverage

Started in the year 1975 on an experimental basis only in 33 blocks, ICDS project has gradually expanded every year. As per the information there are more than 6036 operational projects across the country with 9, 73,767 AWCs against the sanction of

10, 52,638 AWCs.[11] Consequent upon the Eleventh Five-Year Plan approach for universilization of ICDS scheme, Government, by the order,[12] has approved the expansion of AWCs to 14 lakh. This include additional 792 Projects, 2, 13,859 AWCs, 77,012 Mini-AWCs, and an additional provision of 20, 000 Anganwadi for Anganwadi-on-demand. According to official information[13], 13,56, 027 numbers of Anganwadis and Mini-Anganwadis have been sanctioned as on 31.03.2009, out of these 10,33,338 centers are in operation. State-wise number of sanctioned and operational AWCs/Mini AWCs.

Operational Norms

The ICDS scheme guidelines envisage three types of project like;

1. Rural,
2. Urban,
3. Tribal.

The Community Development Blocks in rural areas, Tribal Blocks in tribal areas and Wards/Slums in urban areas is the administrative unit for the location of ICDS project. The sanction of ICDS project and AWC is made according to the population norms that have been revised from time to time. The guidelines prescribed one rural/urban project for 1, 00,000 populations, and one tribal project for 35,000 populations.

Further, one AWC is sanctioned for 1,000 to 1500 population in urban area where as in rural area one AWC is sanctioned for 800 to 1000 populations. In tribal areas one AWC is sanctioned for 500 to 700 populations. Apart from this there is also provision for setting up Mini-AWC in thickly populated areas. In 300 to 500 populated areas, there is a provision for a Mini-AWC.

Community Development Block in the rural area and in the Tribal Block in tribal area was the unit for the sanction of an ICDS project, irrespective of number of villages and population in it. For rural/urban projects, one AWC is sanctioned for 500-1500 population, and one Mini-AWC for 150-500 population. For tribal projects, the population norm was 300-1500 for sanction of one AWC and 150-300 for Mini-AWC. The said population norm has been revised in an order[14] issued by the MWCD of Government of India. As per the revised norms, State has option to opt either more than one project or only one project in a population of more than 2,00,000. For rural/urban projects one AWC is sanctioned for 400-800 population, two AWCs for 800-1600 population, three AWCs for 1600-2400 population. And one Mini-AWC is sanctioned for 150-400 population. For tribal/reverie/desert, hilly, and other difficult areas/projects, the population norm is revised to one AWC for 300-800 population, and one Mini-AWC for 150-300 population.

Mini Anganwadi Center vis-à-vis Anganwadi Center

By virtue of the government order,[15] instruction was given for setting up of Mini-AWC in small hamlets/villages of the Tribal Block with a population between 150-300. Later on, in the context of recommendation of Inter-Ministerial Task Force, Government had revised the population norms and allowed to open mini-AWC also in the rural project. As per the government order[16] one mini-AWC was allowed to be set up in a population of 150-500 in rural projects and 150-300 in tribal projects. Similarly, the population norm was revised to 500-1500 for setting up an AWC in rural and urban projects, and 300-1500 in tribal projects. The population norm for setting up a mini-AWC in rural projects has further revised to 150-400.[17] For a mini-AWC, only an Anganwadi Worker is sanctioned whose honorarium half of the honorarium of AWW is working in a full-fledged AWC. Till the year 2005, only supplementary nutrition service was provided in the mini-AWCs. Fund Allocation ICDS is a centrally sponsored scheme designed by the government of India and implemented through the Government of the States and Union Territories. Government of India provides 100 percent financial assistance for ICDS Schemes (General) that is the operating cost. For Supplementary Nutrition,

GOI provides central assistance @ 50 percent of actual expenditure incurred by the States or 50 percent of the expenditure as per schematic norms whichever is less. No allocation is made to States or Union Territories. Funds are released on the basis of number of Anganwadi Centers, ICDS Projects and beneficiaries. Allocation of central funds for supplementary nutrition has increased from 151920.57 lakh in 2006-07 to 206231.81 lakh in 228161.33 lakh in 2007-08, and further to 228161.33 lakh in 2008-09 financial years. For ICDS (General), central grants to states and union territories has increased from 267941.48 lakh in 2006-07 to 310604.13 lakh in 2007-08 and further to 400648.80 lakh in 2008-09 and it is increasing.

Utilization of ICDS by Children

The National Family Health Survey-3 conducted by International Institute of Population Sciences (IIPS) gives a comprehensive picture about the utilization. All in all, the utilization of ICDS service by children is dismal. The proportion of service utilization by under-3 children and 3-6 year aged children does not vary greatly. 32.5 per cent children of 0-35 months and 33.4 per cent children of 36-71 months have received with any services of AWC. There is lees utilization of ICDS service by the urban children. While 34.8 per cent children of rural and only 23.4 per cent children of urban India have received any services from AWC. Through Anganwadis, 20 per cent of children have received immunization, 26.3 per cent children have received food supplements, and 22.8 per cent children have received pre-school education. Among 3-6 years aged children covered by ICDS, only 14 per cent of them are regularly going and 8.8 per cent are occasionally going to the AWCs for pre-school education. 76.7 per cent pre-school aged are not at all going to AWCs. 3/4th of 0-6 year aged children covered by an AWC did not receive any supplementary food from the center. A major proportion (only 12 per cent) of children has received supplementary foods daily.

Challenges of Early Childhood Care and Education

Despite the initiatives taken by private and public players, ECCE is facing with a lot of challenges in our country, where it is not just day care alone but a dire necessity for overall development of children, observes Sindu Aven. The emerging socio-economic environment in India is driving the need for standardization of quality Early Childhood Care and Education (ECCE). It is also propelled by the efforts of the government towards a fruitful implementation of the RTE Act, the thrust of which is free and quality education to all children. Looking at the current developments, ECCE is seemingly headed for a better future. It is, however, imperative to understand the impending challenges for map effective implementation of the standardized approach for preschools in India.

Given that our society and lifestyle is changing at a startling pace, parents want to provide a relevant foundation to their children's education. The focus of pedagogies is shifting from dishing out inert clones off an assembly line, to producing thinking and dynamic individuals. Teachers today are recognizing the importance of early childhood development, as well as the complementing aspects of individual growth, peer interaction, self-reliance and learning through exploration rather than through evaluation and assessment. This has become central to the teaching system. Accordingly, schools and pre schools across the country are implementing the nuances of these ground-breaking approaches in teaching.

Policy Highlights

Cognitive development: The focus, hence, is on catering to the overall child development rather than academic readiness or cognitive development alone. However, ensuring quality benchmark parameters in preschools undoubtedly aims at up scaling standards through standardization. Unfortunately, when it comes to local customization and administering a curriculum tailored to suit the specific learning needs of a child, standardization of curriculum might come as a challenge. It, however, does not mean focusing on academics alone, but paying equal attention to developing life-skills, offering fun-based exploratory learning activities to the child during his formative years.

Holistic development: How can these factors be taken care of through ECCE? The ECCE Policy brings in the role of the Indian Government to ensure comprehensive holistic development for all children till the age of six years and preparing a child for formal schooling. While the policy looks at initiating reforms and measures, the scope of early childhood program goes far beyond basic literacy programs.

Making children school-ready: In addition to the overall awareness programs on health, hygiene and nutrition, making the child school-ready is equally important. ECCE looks at building social, behavioral and emotional competencies. Helping to develop a mind that is attentive to appropriate and child-centric curriculum, intuitive to perceptions through adherence to life-skills, curious to explore and learn through fun-based exploratory learning activities, and to build a body that works with the correct reflexes in children through activities that develop gross motor skills, ECCE is at the overall grooming of a child.

Quality Care: In India, ECCE initiatives are offered through various public and private centres called Anganwadis, Balwadis, play schools, pre schools, day care centres, crèches, kindergartens, and preparatory schools. ECCE, however, has not yet seen much of consistent quality drive in our country, more so, in the absence of centralized policies and regulatory bodies. The access to ECCE is to be transformed into quality care with optimal hygiene, development, and fun. On one hand, the vast cultural, social, and contextual diversities account for customization and personal care, while on the other, freezing quality benchmarks relies on formulation of standard guidelines, which in itself is a challenge.

Overall development: Given the initiatives that a few of the pioneering private and public players have taken, we have reasons to believe that ECCE is headed for a brighter and better future in our country where it is not just a day care alone but a dire necessity for overall development of children. Of course, certain issues will always remain critical, such as standard audits and compliance with optimal hygiene and infrastructural requirements. While optimal child-teacher ratio should be observed, sensitivity to a child's need for emotional and social development is also important. Interestingly, if we compare the Indian scenario with the global one, we are far from reaching our goal. Early Childhood Care and Education has seen effervescent trends on an international platform. Organizations such as the OMEP (Organization Mondiale pour 'Education Préscolaire), which is an international, non-governmental and non profit-making organization, is working on all aspects of early childhood education and care. It defends and promotes the rights of children to education and care worldwide and supports activities improving accessibility to high quality education and care. Today, India needs initiatives such as OMEP to focus on issues related to Early Childhood Care and Education.[18]

Ensuring quality in early education: Early childhood programmes are playing a major (and increasing) role in young children's lives, even in countries where primary education Systems are still being consolidated. But early education services are often of very variable quality, as are the school classrooms to which children progress. Identifying cost-effective and sustainable ways to improve quality in early childhood and primary classes is a high priority.

Better coordinated pre-school Systems: Even in countries with well developed early education services, transition experiences into first grade are frequently stressful for children and parents because of a lack of communication and coordination between two sectors that are governed by different management structures, organization and financing, professional training, curricula and pedagogy. Ensuring effective coordination of transitions between pre-school and primary classes has been a major ECCE theme amongst the world's richest countries over many decades. Addressing these issues is now a global challenge.

Focusing on the most vulnerable and disadvantaged children: Current arrangements for early childhood care and education appear in many cases to run counter to the requirements for implementing the rights of every child, and are equally incompatible with achieving social equity. While some government services in the countries studied are explicitly intended to be pro-poor, all too often they do not function effectively to achieve that goal in practice. At the same time, the impact of a growing private sector is to reinforce rather than reduce inequities of access to quality education. In order to reverse these trends, governments along with international donors and other agencies have a central role to play.

Emerging Challenges

Early childhood is the phase which spans from the period of conception till eight years of age. All major cognitive, social, emotional and physical development takes place during these early years. According to Prof. Jack P. Shonkoff, Harvard University, "A strong foundation in early childhood lays the groundwork for responsible citizenship, economic prosperity, healthy communities, and successful parenting of the next generation. A weak foundation can seriously undermine the social and economic vitality of the nation." So, investing thoroughly in early childhood is investing in the nation's development. Instruction in the dominant state language often leads to learning and teaching difficulty for children from minor indigenous communities. While mother tongue-based multi lingual programs during the early childhood use the child's first language, allowing the learner adequate scope of understanding in their home-based language, it also creates understanding and participation in the classroom setting. Later on this becomes a platform for learners to gradually transfer skills from the familiar language to the unfamiliar one.[19]

Wrong Policies and Plan of Action of the Government

The issues of early childhood care, education and development find place in the National Policy for Children (1974), National Health Policy (2002), National Nutrition Policy. The National Plan of Action for Children (1992) laid importance on appropriate, and low cost family as well as community intervention for early childhood development. The National Plan of Action for Children (2005) intends to improve the nutritional status of children, to reduce IMR and MMR and to increase immunization coverage. The policy or plan of action fails to achieve the target due to (i) lack of convergence of services and lack of coordination of departments or ministries, (ii) insufficient budget allocation, (iii) lack of periodic monitoring of the progress of plan, (iv) lack of accountability.

Gaps in Different Schemes

The schemes are the fallout of national policy or plan of action. The Integrated Child Development Services (ICDS) schemes had emerged in 1975 in order to give effect to the National Policy for Children (1974). ICDS is the only comprehensive scheme in the country that cater the need of ECCE. The Supreme Court of India in a writ Petition of People's Union of Civil Liberties (PUCL) vs. Union of India views that ICDS schemes is covered under the schemes relating to the right to food. The components under the National Rural Health Mission (NRHM) and Sarva Shiksha Abhiyan (SSA) are also potential to provide support to the ECCE even though its primary responsibility lies with the ministry of health and ministry of education respectively while ICDS comes under the ministry of women and child development.

Universalisation of ICDS with quality has been the direction of the Supreme Court of India and this has found place in the National Common Minimum Programmes as a core commitment of United Progressive Alliance Government headed by Dr. Manmohan Singh, the then Prime-Minister of India. To quote a study report "in concrete terms," 'universalisation with quality' would mean that –

(1) Every settlement has an AWC,

(2) All ICDS services are extended to all children under the age of six years and all eligible women and girls,

(3) The quality of services is radically improved and

(4) Priority should be given to disadvantaged groups, especially residents of Scheduled Castes and Scheduled Tribes, hamlets and urban slums. ECCE requires strategic intervention on child care, health, nutrition and education; present ICDS schemes lacks either in infrastructure or in delivery of services.

- According to a report of HAQ: Centre for Child Rights, ICDS has not yet reached to every poor young child despite its existence since 1975. Services under ICDS schemes covered only 3.41 crore children in the age group of 0-6 years which is around 22 percent of the total children in that age group. Supplementary Nutrition too is currently provided to 3.77 crore children, as opposed to 16 crore children of whom 47 percent are reported to be undernourished.
- The coverage of ICDS is highly inadequate. There are 10 lakh AWC in the country as against the requirement of minimum 18 lakh for universal coverage based on the existing norms. The Eleventh Five Year Plan has proposal to increase the AWC to 14 lakh.
- The infrastructure facilities of AWC remain very poor. According to Rapid Facility Survey of Infrastructure at nearly three lakh Anganwadi Centres conducted by the National Council of Applied Economic Research (NCAER) in 2012, more than 40 percent of AWCs are neither housed in a ICDS building nor in a rented building and more than 45 percent did not have toilet facilities, while 27 percent did not have the basic drinking water facilities.
- The amount sanctioned for expenditure for providing ICDS services, especially on supplementary nutrition to children, women and adolescent girls, remains unspent in most of the states. States spent a meager amount per day providing

supplementary nutrition in defiance to the Supreme Court order of spending Rupees Two per day in catering supplementary nutrition to children.

- There is lack of convergence between the core programmes of ICDS with NRHM, SSA, and Drinking Water & Sanitation Programmes.
- One of the services of ICDS is health service which comes under the Ministry of health. Treatment of malnourished children is of joint responsibility of the ICDS and Health Department, hardly any coordination between the two is visible in the micro level.
- There is overburden of work in AWC for a single Anganwadi worker for which the services, particularly pre-school education, are greatly hampered.
- There is no convergence of day-care centers or crèches in the Anganwadi Centres for providing care and services to the children whose mothers go for work outside the home and there is no adult care taker at the home.
- Proper attention is not given for the training, capacity building and orientation of Anganwadi workers.
- Planning process of ICDS is not decentralized as a result attention is not given to the tribal culture, language and style of living.

Financial Crunch and Political Will

Very often the implementation of programmes and plan of actions are hampered due to insufficient budget allocation. Low budgetary allocations have been one of the key factors responsible for the limited impact of the ICDS and related programmes so far. According to a report of HAQ: Center for Child Rights, only one percent of the total union budget is spent on children under six years of age. The allocations for ICDS has increased from Rs. 1490.40 crore in 2004-05 to Rs. 3142.25 crore in the 2010-11 budget. But this increase is no way sufficient to cover the required cost of universal coverage of all 17 lakh habitations in the country.

For the fair implementation of ECCE framework including the universal coverage of ICDS, maternity entitlements, crèches and supplementary nutrition for adolescent girls, budgetary allocation should be increased. According to a recent analysis of parliamentary proceedings by HAQ, only three percent of the questions raised in Parliament during the last four years related to children. Further, among the child-related questions, less than 5 percent were concerned with child care and development in the age group of zero to six years.

Lack of Statutory Back-up to Article-45 of the Constitution of India

The provisions under the Directive Principles of State Policy require the law-making organ of the state is to make law for the implementation of the principles. This has been given to understand that number of laws have been made by the union parliament to give effects to many of the provisions of Directive Principles of State Policy. The notable of them are, Minimum Wages Act and Equal Remuneration Act to give effect to proviso of Article-39 and 43 relating to the equality of right to men and women to an adequate means of livelihood, and equal pay for equal work for both men and women, living wage for workers; Legal Services Authority Act for Article-39(A) concerning equal justice and free legal aid, Maternity Benefit Act for Article-42 concerning provision for human condition of works and maternity relief and Protection of Environment and Wildlife Act for giving effect to Article-48(A) concerning protection and improvement of environment and safeguarding of forest and wildlife. Looking at the principles of Constitution, formulation and enactment of a law on ECCE is of the responsibility of the state for giving effect to the Article-45, what is very much lacking in the present.

Measuring the Effects of ECCE on School Retention and Learning Achievement

Good quality early childhood education programme has productive value. It helps the children to develop readiness for primary schooling in terms of social, physical, academic and cognitive readiness. Research in India also provides evidence of the short and long term benefits of god quality early childhood care and education programme.

Unlike the government school, it is essential in private and public school (English Medium Schools) that the child who come for admission in Standard-I, he/she should have got 3 years of pre-school education, i.e. Pre-Nursery, Nursery, LKG, & UKG. It is well proved that children with experience of pre-school education are likely to perform better in next level of education and their learning level would be higher as compared to children without pre-school education. This statement has been substantiated in the study report of PRATHAM titled 'Annual Status of Education Report (Rural) Nationally, among the Class-I students, 34.9 per cent can read nothing, 41.9 per cent can read letter, 16.4 per cent can read word, and only 4.1 per cent can read Level-I (Standard-I) text. Only 15.1 per cent of Class-II, 28.1 per cent of Class-III, 28.6 per cent of Class-IV, and 24.6 per cent of Class-V students can read Standard-I text. While more than 75 per cent of Class-V students of private school can read at least Level-2 (Standard –II) text, this can be read by only 56.2 per cent of government school Class-V students. Among the Standard-III students of private school, 50 per cent of them can do subtraction as compared 33.2 per cent of government school students. Only 37 per cent of Standard-V government school students can do at least division, whereas 50 per cent of private school students can do this.

Conclusion

The potential of quality early childhood care and education (ECCE) to transform young lives is increasingly recognized. Accounts of innovative and effective programmes have been disseminated widely and endorsed by scientific evidence as well as economic and human rights arguments. Reports about model programmes and the high returns on ECCE investments provide crucial leverage in advocating for policy change and programme development. They are also a source of inspiration to all who work with children and families. But they tell only part of the story. This early childhood stage is also important as a foundation for the inculcation of social and personal habits and values that are known to last a life time. Given this wide scope, early childhood development has been defined and described in various ways under various programmes. The nomenclature and definition include Early Childhood Education Programmes, which are preschool education focused. Programes 3-6 year's olds as seen in nurseries, kindergartens, preparatory schools, etc. Early Childhood Care and Education (ECCE) retains the same educational thrust but enlarges its scope to include the care component including care and early stimulation for 0-3 years old, through crèches and home based parent education. ECCE plays significant role as it helps children in successful completion of primary education. Research studies have also shown that ECCE education enhance literacy skills, child ability to learn, to communicate ideals and feelings and to get along well with others children who receive quality ECCE are more likely to succeed in school and in life.

Good pre-school education increase cognitive abilities, school achievement, improve class room behavior, decrease grade repetition among children. The ECCE is therefore an integral part of child rearing experience provided by an agency for all children. One of the providers of ECCE in India is Integrated Child Development Services (ICDS) network. The ECCE is one of the components of ICDS programme. An attempt has been made to critically examine the ECCE services through ICDS programme challenges thereof.

The situational analysis of the state of early childhood care and education in India with reference to constitutional provision of Article-45, policies and schemes relating to young children, programmatic interventions, and 11th Five-Year Plan approach indicates that early childhood care and education is not recognized as a right of children. While early childhood care and education is a privilege for the children of affluent and elite parents, many children of poor, marginalized and disadvantaged communities are being deprived of getting opportunity to receive ECCE. The very important aspect of ECCE is pre- primary education, which enables the child to develop readiness for primary education. Following the incorporation of ECCE in Article-45 of Directive Principles of Indian Constitution, government has recognized early childhood care and education as a core issue for holistic development of the child. In order to translate the constitutional principles in practice, government of India has integrated early childhood care and education in the form of non-formal pre-school education in the Integrated Child Development Services (ICDS) scheme. Even though ICDS programme is conceptually holistic, comprehensive and integrated, the pre-school education service is either poorly implemented or almost neglected.

The problems lie with the policy approach as early childhood care and education is not integrated with the education. ICDS programme does not have the balance linkage between health, nutrition and pre-primary education. ICDS is a programme of basic health (i.e. immunization, health check-up) and supplementary feeding rather than a programme for early childhood education (i.e. pre-primary education). From policy approach to actual implementation, there are plenty of problems ICDS particularly related to pre-school activities. Pre-school education at Anganwadi centers is hampered largely due to;

(i) Lack of basic infrastructure (i.e. building, space, play & game materials, learning kits),

(ii) Untrained or inadequately trained pre-school instructor (AWW),

(iii) Absence of standard pre-school curriculum indicating learning methods for pre-school activities, language to be used for communication;

(iv) Lack of monitoring and supervision;

(v) Absence of community participation.

References

1. Annual Report (2006-07): Ministry of Tribal Affairs; Government

of India, Report of Ministry of Women & Child Development; Government of India.

2. Care & Protection of Young Children under Juvenile Justice Act (2000).
3. Census of India (2011).
4. *Children with parental Care*, A CLAP Publication, Dr. Bikash Das, President of Committee for Legal Aid to Poor.
5. Early Childhood Care and Education; An introduction, Romila Soni, Rajendra Kapoor and Krishnakant Vashistha, National Council of Educational Research Training.
6. Importance of ECCE, Pramod Kishore Acharya, Senior Researcher, NLUO.
7. National Family Health Survey Report.
8. Plan India: ECCD: Sustaining Early Childhood Interventions.
9. Rajiv Gandhi National Crèche Scheme for the Children of Working/ Ailing Mothers.
10. UNESCO: Education for All Global Monitoring Report (2007).
11. UNICEF: Progress for Children; A World Fit for Children Statistical Review (Number 6, December 2007).
12. United Nations Convention on the Rights of the Child.
13. Walter Barker: Early Childhood Care & Education: The Challenge; Bernard van Leer Foundation.
14. Working Group on Children Under Six: Strategies for Children Fewer than Six Published in Economic & Political Weekly, December 29, 2007.

Notes

1. Census-2011 (as on March 01, 2011,-http://censusindia.gov.in)
2. Early Childhood Care and Education, by M. Sen Gupta.
3. Rights of the Child under Indian Constitution
4. www.indg.in/.../policiesandschemes/the-national-policy-on-children-1974
5. National Policy on Education, 1986.

6. http://www.wcd.nic.in, Minister of State for Human Resource Evelopment (Department of Women & Child Development) Government of India, New Delhi.
7. The Pre-Natal Diagnostic Techniques (Regulation and Prevention of Misuse) Act, 1994 (Act No. 57 of 1994) and The Pre-Natal Diagnostic Techniques (Regulation and Prevention of Misuse) Amendment Act, 2002 (No.14 Of 2003).
8. Report of the working groups on Child rights for the 12th Five Year Plan-2012-2017.
9. Department of Elementary Education & Learning, MHRD, GOI; 2001.
10. No.4-4/2008-CD-II, dated 11 May 2009, MWCD, GOI
11. Annual Report (2007-08) MWCD, GOI.
12. No. F. 14– 1/2008-CD-1, dated 18 November 2008, MWCD, GOI.
13. Information provided by the MWCD, GOI under RTI Act, 2005.
14. No. F. 14– 1/2008-CD-1, dated 18 November 2008, MWCD, GOI.
15. No. 1-9/96-CDI dated 25 June 1996, MWCD, GOI.
16. No. 1-5/2004-CDI dated 15 March 2007, MWCD, GOI.
17. No. F. 14– 1/2008-CD-1, dated 18 November 2008, MWCD, GOI.
18. http://www.deccanherald.com/content/360703/challenges-early-childhood-care.html
19. Emerging Challenges of Early Childhood Care and Education (ECCE) Through ICDS in India, Dr. Pinki Malik.

5

Early Childhood Care and Education: Theory and Practice

The concept of Early Childhood Care (ECE), or Early Childhood Education (ECE), Early Childhood Care and Education (ECCE), or Early Childhood Care and Development (ECCD) has been used in different context, the thrust of each nomenclature is almost identical, and same i.e. the holistic development of the child in a right based approach.[1]

Early childhood period is a vital period in every individual's life. It is also a vital period of human development, when a rapid development of human brain and also a formative stage for inculcation of social values and culture takes place in the child. It is a stimulating period for the child for the concept formation, vocabulary identification, and language acquisition and development. As multiple developments take place in early childhood period, it is always logical to make more investment in the programs related to early childhood care, education and development.

The Early Childhood Care and Education (ECCE) programme gained more importance today. Driven by various socio-economic compulsions these days both parents seek jobs and remain away from the child for the whole day. Early Childhood Care centre provide them a safer alternative where their children can grow and develop in a simulative environment. Therefore, ECCE has been comprehensively included in teacher training Programmes at all levels.[2]

This chapter measures the legal status of early childhood care and education in India, which was inculcated under Article-45 of the Constitution of India, and it focus on the rudiments of ECCE. The importance of ECCE in securing education across the childhood has been devised in various research documents and well spelt in various international conferences. The worldwide extensive researches reveals that appropriate care and education, during the years before a child reaches the age of formal schooling, has lasting effect on their intellectual capacity, personality and social behavior.

It is recognized that children who have received qualitative early childhood care and education, show better school readiness, higher school attendance, and better performance. World Conferences on Education for All held in 1990 at Jometin of Thailand upholds the crucial importance of early childhood education by reaffirming the phrase "Learning begins at birth" and adopting the statement that, "the pre-condition of educational quality, equity, and efficiency are set in the early childhood years, making to early childhood care and development essential to the achievement of basic educational goals." As the follow-up to the Jometin WCEFA, number of conferences were held such as Second Education for All Forum in New Delhi in 1993, Education for All Summit of Nine High Population Countries held in New Delhi in 1993, European Policy Conference on Early Childhood Education in Amsterdam in 1998, where various aspects of ECCE was discussed and ECE framework was designed.

The deliberations of world leaders and country representatives made in all these conferences have succeeded in placing the subject matter of ECCE as a primary agenda in the education framework. In the global context, the Darkar Framework of Action adopted in the World Education Forum, 2000 is the most important event in education. The framework views for the expansion and improvement in the ECCE service as it makes children ready for formal education, reduces dropout rate and reduces delayed enrolment.

Early childhood care and education has become a key issue in social science as well as in politics. In many countries, different actors increasingly use the concept of early childhood programs to tackle a variety of societal challenges. This contributes theoretical and empirical dimensions to a body of research that has neglected a number of questions to date.

(1) The effects of early childhood care and education on the development of children from different social backgrounds,

(2) Socio cultural disparities in the use of childcare services.[3]

Aims and Objectives of ECCE

The Early Childhood Care and Education students should be able to identify and discuss the nutritional, social, emotional, cognitive, and physical and health needs of the child. More importantly they should be able to display and apply the knowledge and competencies acquired in appropriate situations.

Specifically the care-givers/teacher should be able to:

- Assist the child to develop good eating habits.
- Assist the child to develop good social habits.
- Facilitate emotional stability in the child.
- Assist the child to develop communication, reasoning and expressive skills.
- Assist the child to develop fine and gross motor skills,
- Assist the child to develop good health habits with emphasis on sanitation and safety needs.
- Assist the child to develop inquisitiveness and to explore his/her environment.
- Utilize the resources and improvise materials to stimulate the child through play.
- Keep records of the child's developmental progress in terms of major mile stones.
- Identify children with special needs for referrals.
- Discuss the needs, progress and development of the child with parents and caregivers.

- Assist the child to acquire desirable attributes e.g. good morals, norms and values.
- Participate actively in professional associations/organizations relevant to Early Childhood Care and Education and Manifest desirable administrative competence in Early Childhood Care and Education.

ECCE: History and Development

Although the concept of the Early Childhood Care & Education (ECCE) activities has received a worldwide attention and expanded in a large extent since 1990, the concept of ECCE is not of recent origin. The philosophy of ECCE (some where referred as Early Childhood Care & Development), as a concept or principle, has a long history. The chronology of theoretical development can be traced back to the period of philosophical work of greatest Greek Philosophers like Plato and Aristotle, Emanuel Kant, fitches etc.

The significance of ECCE has been deliberated in the philosophy of J.A. Comenius, John Locke, J.J. Rousseau, J.H. Pestalozzi, F.A. Froebel, John Dewey, and Jean Piaget. In the 18th century, Europe had plenty of early childhood advocates who stressed on the importance of a child's first seven years of life. However, the importance of educating poor children did not gain much needed attention until the early 19th century when Robert Owen provided poor children with opportunities for education and societal improvements. Later on Pestalozzi advocated for education of all categories of children including the poor children. As a result, conceptions of childhood changed from that of a miniature adult to that of a child with rights, the right to learn through play.[4] Consequently, new teaching methods had emerged focusing on child development, appropriate curriculum and learning.

During the period of 1960s, when the civil rights and women's rights movement gets momentum efforts, it had a tremendous impact on the nature of early childhood programmes and that also highlighted the importance of educating disadvantaged children. With the advancement of Science and technology, rapid growth of industrialization, urbanization and modernization, a good size of female population has entered into the workforce. The working women have added responsibility of worker in addition to the traditional role of mother and house wife. In the crunch of multiple responsibilities, they, more often, find difficulties in taking proper care of their kids. Hence, demand for institutional childcare got the way. Further, the demise of traditional systems of childcare and breakdown of extended (joint) family support systems has augmented a growing demand for quality early childhood programmes. Till the last quarter of the 20th century, demand for institutional childcare was restricted only for the children of working women.

Since the 1980s, the early childhood education (ECCE) has been defined as the education of young children from birth to the age group of six years.[5] This wide age range has shown a growing debate and a lack of consensus as to what type of programme is most appropriate. Typically, the ECCE programmes contain several age related areas ranging from infancy, pre-school, kindergarten, and primary grades. Such programmes not only vary by age but by characteristics of the child in each stage. Various researchers have found both short as well as long-term outcomes of ECCE programmes[6] and have also shown that children from low-income families who are covered under ECCE Programmes get lot of benefits.[7] Significant short-term benefits were evident on children's Intelligence Quotient (IQ). As for long-term gains, children were more successful in areas of school achievement.[8]

ECCE programmes have also been associated with positive outcomes in cognitive, social, and emotional development in children.[9] With the adoption of the United Nations Convention on the Rights of the Child (UNCRC) by the United Nations General Assembly on November 20, 1989, the international drive for expanding ECE Programmes began. Semblance to international efforts, World Conference on Education for All was held in

Jomtien, Thailand in 1990 where delegates from 155 countries, as well as representatives from some 150 organizations adopted the World Declaration on Education for All. In Article-5, the Declaration has endorsed the philosophy 'learning begins from birth' and broadened the scope of basic education. It also prioritized ECCE as a foundation for later learning and development. This World Conference has really instigated the signatory countries to incorporate the ECCE service in policy-making agenda and to make variety arrangements involving families, communities or institutional programmes.

The objective of EFA, a World Conference on Special Needs Education was held in Spain in 1994. Representatives from 92 Governments and 25 International Organizations of the world called for inclusion Early Childhood Care and Education programmes for children aged up to six years taking into account the important role of Early Childhood Care and Education. The ECCE programmes ought to be developed to promote physical, intellectual and social development and school readiness of children. Later, the World Education Forum in Dakar 2000 which included 1,100 participants from 164 countries adopted the Dakar Framework for Action, reviewed the advances made in basic education in the 1990s, and strengthened the commitment to achieve quality basic education for all by 2015. In addition, it focused attention on the world's youngest children where they became a global agenda for EFA by 2000 through setting specific goals for them.

The first specific goal of the Darkar Framework for Action called for expanding and improving comprehensive Early Childhood Care and Education, especially for the most vulnerable and disadvantaged children.

Physical Development: Concerning the physical growth, development and control of the body.

Perception and Sensory Development: Concerning development of sense and ability to process the information.

Communication and Language Development: Concerning the use of visual and sound stimuli for the acquisition of language, exchange of thoughts and feelings.

Cognitive Development: Concerning the manner of individual thinking and reaction to the situation.

Emotional Development: Concerning children's increasing awareness and control of their feelings and how does he/she react to these feelings in a given situation.

Social Development: Concerning the child's identity, their relationship with others, and understanding their place within a social environment.

The Consultative Groups on ECCD has laid the following principles of child development.

Development is holistic and consists of inter-dependent dimensions: This means that the child's development cannot be compartmentalized into health, nutrition, and education, social, emotional and spiritual variables. All are interwoven in a child's life and are developing simultaneously. Progress in one area affects progress in others. Similarly, when something goes wrong in any one of those areas, it has an impact on all the other areas.

Development begins pre-natally and learning occurs at birth: The chemistry of the child, i.e. the physical construction, and brain development starts from the moment of conception. These all have an impact on child's ability to learn, to thrive, to grow and be healthy. The first 6 years of a child's life form the foundation for all later development; early attention to the child's needs is very critical. Developmental psychologists have demonstrated that in the early years a child develops all the basic brain and physiological structures upon which later growth and learning are dependent. Children's needs differ across the early childhood years. The developmental needs of the child usually vary in relation to the maturation process in the following stages.

Development is multi-determined, and varies as a function of the child's nutritional and biomedical status, genetic

inheritance, and social and cultural context: There is a general pattern or sequence for development of children. The character and quality of development vary from child to child as a result of what the child brings into the world (the child's nature) and the experiences the child has in the world (nurture). Culture influences development in different ways. It is important for adults to use methods that fit with the child's growth pattern, not only in the cognitive (intellectual) area, but also in the emotional, perceptual and motor areas.

Children's development is cumulative in nature: If children's early nutrition and health are jeopardized, then development is delayed or debilitated, and, over time the child's development follows a downward trajectory. As a result, some children fall further and further behind their peers. The earlier attention is given to children's health, nutritional and developmental status, the better. If interventions are going to be provided only after the age of three, there may be limits on what can be achieved in terms of overcoming already existing deficits resulting from poor nutrition, illness and neglect. If adequate care is provided in the first three years, then there can be some very positive long-term outcomes from programs that focus on the pre-school years.

Children are active participants in their own development and learning. Learning involves the child's construction of knowledge, not an adult's imposition of information. It is important for children to have opportunities to construct their own knowledge through exploration, interaction with materials and imitation of role models. Children need opportunities to learn by doing, to be engaged in problem solving, and to develop language and communication skills. Opportunities for active involvement should abound, whether at home in everyday chores or in more organized settings outside the home. Emphasis should be on how to learn (i.e., positive attitudes toward learning and thinking skills) rather than on what to learn. Development and learning occur as a result of the child interacting with people and objects in his or her environment. Children need opportunities to interact with peers, adults and objects in a safe environment that provides the child with security and acceptance. Learning and development can be fostered by creating a healthy environment, and providing space, materials and opportunities to help children to learn through play, whether at home or elsewhere. Children live within a context– family, community, culture and their needs are most effectively addressed in relation to that context.

The child's well being is closely linked to the well-being of the family, specifically to the well-being of the primary caregiver(s). Therefore, support to the family and community can help children; similarly support to children can help the family and community. Since the environment has an impact on children's development, it is also possible to develop interventions that make changes in the child's environment.

Prenatal and Birth: During this period, attention is focused on the mother through maternal and child health programs, and parental support and education.

Infancy (up to about 18 months): Particular emphasis needs to be placed on health and nutrition during this period. Breastfeeding is critical; every attempt should be made for children to be with their mothers. Sensory learning, especially auditory and visual, control of physical actions, and attachment to a significant caregiver seem to be the central tasks.

Toddler and Post-toddler (about 18 to 36 months): During this period nutrition continues to be critically important. A child's coordination, language, ability to think and social skills advance rapidly.

Pre-school (from 3-5 or 6 years): In the pre-school years, socialization and preparation for schooling take on greater importance, and the circle of peers and caregivers widens. From age four onward, early childhood programs are more likely to be associated with education and pre schools, but health and nutrition remain key components of what young children need. Early primary school, a period of "transition" into school.

Philosophy of Early Childhood Care and Education

The early years (0-6) are crucial for the development of an individual and any support given at this stage helps to promote the development of the child. This period requires people who are knowledgeable, such as specialist care givers and teachers. Such people should be equipped for the task, hence the need to train them in ECCE to be able to handle these children effectively. Caregivers and teacher of young children therefore, should possess such qualities as enthusiasm, kindness, gentleness and tolerance. In addition they should possess academic and professional qualifications, Nigeria Certificate in Education (NCE). The principles and practices of modern early childhood education have their origins from the philosophy of great political thinkers, psychologists, educationists, and sociologists. Here is presented the views of some noted thinkers.

Johan Amos Comenius (1592-1670)[10]

Joham Amos Comenius, a Moravian Bishop, is one of the founders of modern early childhood education who believed in social reform through education. His General Postulates of Teaching and Learning, which appeared in his immortal classic called The *Great Didactic* (1657), can be considered one of the first descriptions of a system of education designed specifically for young children. He firmly stressed on learning through the direct experience of senses because sense impressions would be internalized and stored for future interpretation. To him, "the acquisition of knowledge is essentially based on the activities followed by reasoning. The idea of symbolic learning of Comenius was later applied by Rudolph and Cohen (1964) in kindergarten curriculum. Even though Comenius believed in individual differences among children, he propounded for Education to All irrespective of gender or social standard.

John Locke (1632-1704)

John Locke applied the scientific laws of his time to human

development, believing that it proceeded according to specific laws. He believed that a person was not person at birth, but developed as a result of encounters with the environment. Locke believed that the individual was a blank slate who re-ceived impressions from the environment via the senses, and that these impressions should be part of education. He placed strong emphasis on physical activity, believing in "a sound mind in a sound body," and felt that the family was respon-sible for education and so provided guidelines for parents. English thinker John Locke insisted both that children are potentially free and rational beings, and that the realization of these crucial human qualities tends to be thwarted through imposition of the sort of prejudice that perpetuates oppression and superstition.

Locke believed, upbringing and education that stymied development of children's humanity when the older generation, itself enmeshed in prejudice, preferred to maintain the status quo rather than to examine whether their lives qualified as truly human through the rational and free action characteristic of autonomous individuals.[11]

Jean-Jacques Rousseau (1712-1778)

Rousseau's publication of Emile in 1762 called "attention to the importance of the early childhood years" and changed the history of education. Rousseau suggested that the young children are in of need motor activity, first hand experiences, and happy games to develop language, mathematical and sensory concepts. He believed in the natural goodness of children and opposed the artificial life style of the times. He suggested that young children be protected from society and allowed to engage in activities that were natural for children. Children should be allowed to become fully developed or mature before exposing them to society.

The children should have the freedom to play and be spontaneous. He advocated a study of how children develop at different ages as the basis for educational practice. Rousseau proposed that formal learning activities be delayed until age 12 and suggested that educators use motivating activities to ensure attention and interest. He believed that young children should gain self-acceptance and discipline from the natural consequences of things and activities. Rousseau's naturalism emphasized freedom, growth, interest, and activity as the basis for early education.[12]

Friedrich Wilhelm Froebel (1782-1852)

According to Froebel childhood is a unique time and learning is an active process, the inclusion of play is an educational method. He suggested a cooperative social environment rather than a competitive environment and put forth the belief that education might be a process of unfolding of abilities. He propounded for a child centered education curriculum, which should include self-activity, physical activity, music, outdoor activities, and a series of manipulative materials called "Gifts and Occupations." He advocated for the training of the young women teachers and for the development of songs and finger- plays both at home and in schools.

John Dewey (1859-1952)

The philosophy of John Dewey had greatly helped to transform the role of the kindergarten at the turn of the twentieth century and eventually influenced the entire field of early childhood education. He was in favor of community classroom teaching where child learns in cooperation with each other. He promoted teacher flexibility, creativity, and responsibility and the introduction of art and music, field trips, and nature studies, to encourage problem solving and independent thinking. He considered classroom as a Model and teachers as a Guide. Children usually involved with such activities that have a purpose. When children are exposed to right type of materials and role models, they develop skills for later academic learning as well as flexibility to cope with social and emotional problems. Dewey, more than anyone else, is associated with the alternative to traditional education known as child-or learner-centered education. Dewey's contribution to education was part and parcel of his contribution to shaping the intellectual life of the time in which he lived.[13]

Jean Piaget (1896-1980)

The legacy of Jean Piaget to the world of early childhood education is that he fundamentally altered the view of how a child learns and a teacher, he believed, was more than a transmitter of knowledge. He was also an essential observer and guide to helping children build their own knowledge. Piaget's continued interactions with young children became part of his life-long research.[14]

Piaget developed an influential theory relating to the process and manner of child thinking. His theory of intellectual development contains the following:

- Infancy is recognized as a critical period in cognitive development.
- Child is considered as an active participant in the learning pro-cess from birth.
- Cognitive development is divided into four distinct stages through which children go in a specific sequence at their own rate which is influenced by experience and maturation.
- Change in the role of the teacher from an imparter of information to a designer of activities appropriate to a child's level of development.

His theory provided a means by which children's levels of intellectual functioning, intellectual readiness, and the appropriateness of classroom activities can be assessed. Piaget provided a new way of viewing the importance of the early years in the life of the child as the foundation for later learning.

Maria Montessori (1870-1952)

She had developed a child-centered approach to education known as Montessori method. She viewed that child develops from within as an individual.[15] Child should be free to select and use materials with a minimum adult interference. Montessori advocated a change in the role of the teacher from a shaper of behavior to an observer of child development and the development of independence, self-care, and self-confidence through self-directed activities in an unhurried environment that was suited to the needs of the child. Her philosophy to education is based on the following:

- Children as natural learners.
- Instruction of children in 3-year age groups, corresponding to sensitive periods of development.
- Children as competent beings, encouraged to make maximal decisions.
- Observation of the child in the environment as the basis for ongoing curriculum development.
- Small, child sized furniture and creation of a small, child-sized environment (microcosm) in which each can be competent to produce overall a self-running small children's world.
- Creation of a scale of sensitive period of development, which provides a focus for class work that, is appropriate and uniquely stimulating and motivating to the child

The importance of the "absorbent mind," the limitless motivation of the young child to achieve competence over his or her environment and to perfect his or her skills and understandings as they occur within each sensitive period.

Theories of Early Childhood Care and Education

There are three sets of interdisciplinary theories – Behaviorist Theory, Maturations Theory, Stage Theory and Constructivism Theory – where reference is made to Early Childhood Care (ECC), Early Childhood Education (ECE), Early Childhood Behavior (ECB), Early Childhood Development, and Early Childhood Learning (ECL). Each theory sets a philosophy for the selection of school curriculum. The behaviorists propounded for the use of direct Instruction Methods in school curriculum.[16] The Constructivists have opined for High-Scope Curriculum and Creative Curriculum. Developed in the United States of America in 1960 and being used in other countries of the world, the High-Scope Curriculum is a method for running of nursery school or

Kindergarten. In High-Scope method, children are the active learner and adults working with children are seen as only facilitator rather than manger or supervisor. The method of learning in High-Scope Institution is play like method. There must be separate space for different play and child should have independent access to all the facilities. The most important part of the High-Scope Approach is the 'Plan-do-Review Sequence' in which children first plan what they want to play with and how they want to play.

The by-product of Maturation theory is the Montessori approach of educational method for children. This method is applied in pre-schools and elementary schools. This method is characterized by an emphasis on self-directed activity on the part of the child and clinical observation on the part of the teachers. It stresses on the importance of adapting child's learning environment to his developmental level, and the role of physical activity in absorbing academic concepts and practical skills. Another approach, i.e. Reggio Emilia Approach has been developed which is a mixture of Constructivist Theory and Maturationist Theory. The philosophy of Reggio Emilia Approach is for natural development of children where child must have control over his/her day-to-day activity. Parents are viewed as the vital component. In fact they are seen as partners, collaborators, and advocates for their children. Teacher should respect each parents as the child first teacher and involve parents in every aspect of the curriculum.

Constructivist Theory

The Constructivism otherwise called as Jean Piaget and Lev Vygotsky advocated Learning Theory. Jean Piaget (1896-1980) Swiss philosopher, natural scientist, and developmental psychologist, is well known for his work studying children, his theory of cognitive development, and epistemological view called "Genetic Epistemology". Current theoretical and practical conceptualizations in the field of early childhood special education are limited in their attention to the socio cultural context in which development occurs.

This is argued for a paradigmatic shift away from the individualistic models of development and learning to a social constructivist model that stems from views of learning and development.[17] He divided the cognitive development process into four stages that correspondence to –

(1) Infancy,

(2) Pre-School,

(3) Childhood,

(4) Adolescence.

The four development stages are described in Piaget Theory as:

Sensory-Motor Stage: From birth to the age of 2 years. During this stage the child experiences the world through movement as well as senses and learns object permanence.

Pre-Operational Stage: From 2 years to 7 years. In this stage, the child acquires motor skills.

Concrete Operational Stage: From 7 to 11 years. During this stage, the child begins to think logically about the concrete objects.

Formal Operational Stage: From 11 years onwards. This stage is characterized by development of abstract reasoning.

Each stage is characterized by general cognitive structure which affects the thinking process of the child. Development from one stage to next is continuous and if there are any accumulation errors, there would be cognitive disequlibrium in the subsequent stages of development. Piaget considered children as *little philosophers*, and scientists who build their own individual theories of knowledge. The transition between the stages tends to be rapid and radical. Each new stage is created through the further differentiation, integration, and synthesis of the new structure out of the old. Hence, the sequence of cognitive stages is logically necessary, rather than simply empirically correct. Piaget advocated that through the process of objectification, reflection and abstraction, the child may construct the principles on which action is not only effective or correct but also *justified.*

Lev Semenovich Vygotsky (1896-1934)

Soviet Developmental Psychologist was the founder of cultural-historical psychology. He investigated the role of culture and interpersonal communication for child development. He viewed that the development of mental function occurs when within the particular cultural groups, as well as at the individual level through the social interactions with significant people in a child life, particularly the parents. Through these interactions, a child becomes able to learn the habits of mind of her/his culture, including speech patterns, written language, and other symbolic knowledge. This key approach of Vygotsky is often referred to as *Cultural Mediation*. The specific knowledge gained by child through these interactions also represented the shared knowledge of a culture. This process is known as Internalization.

Lev Semenovich Vygotsky (1896–1934) is best known for his theories of cognitive development in which he explored the importance of culture, language development, and the use of cognitive apprenticeships in the classroom.[18]

Cognitive Development and Education of Young Children

This concept is about how the cognitive development of young children can be affected by early childhood programs. It therefore does not describe "everything" that psychologists know or believe about cognitive development in young children. According to his guiding assumption that early childhood education is not about young children as such, but about how teachers and children form *relationships* that mutually influence each other and that especially influence children. As a teacher, he will often do more than this, of course he may engage children in further activities that extend their interests, motives, and abilities.

By giving this perspective and given a focus on the needs of early childhood educators, certain theories and topics about human change and functioning get "promoted" in value to the exclusion of others. As a rule, theories that highlight social influence or collaborative processes are more useful to teachers of young children than viewpoints that leave human interaction out of the picture.[19] Pretend play is especially important to educators working with the youngest children and who seek to provide them with the most developmentally appropriate practice possible. As it turns out, pretend play also clearly supports the claim that cognitive development in early childhood is "really" social. The benefits of this people-oriented activity are very real, but definitely not confined to the social. The cognitive skills are ones that early childhood teacher's value and those they can encourage deliberately. Cognitive development refers to the development of a child in terms of information processing, conceptual resources, perceptual skill and language.

Key Points: The brain grows and matures rapidly during the early childhood period as faster than any other organ in a child's body. Through a process known as synaptic pruning, neurons that are not useful to the brain die off, making room for more relevant connections to help a child to learn. Piaget's preoperational and concrete operational define the development of childhood. The preoperational stage focuses on the development of concept through make-believe play and development of symbolism. The concrete operational stage allows a child's thinking to become more logical and focused. Several key thinking processes emerge during this phase, including reversibility, serration, and transitive inference. Reversibility is the capacity to go through a series of steps and mentally reverse them, ending up back at the beginning.

The Brain: The brain grows and matures rapidly during early childhood, faster than any other organ in a child's body. Once nerve cells in the brain are in place, they form synapses. These synapses release neuro transmitters, which are chemical signals that help the brain communicate. Synapses evolve rapidly, and in doing so, some synapses will die off to make room for new or more important ones. The developing brain will grow from 30 percent of its adult weight at birth to 70 percent by age 2 due to synaptic pruning, myelination and a child's environmental experiences.

Piaget's Childhood Stages: Piaget's preoperational and concrete operational define the development of childhood. During these stages, growth and development occur to assist the child in further development. According to Piaget, each stage of development incorporates previous knowledge; that is, a child needs to go through an earlier stage in order to fully develop in a later stage.

Preoperational development allows a child to increase his or her mental representation of objects, generally through make-believe play. Piaget states that language is the most flexible means of mental representation, but that children do not yet have the capability to solely use language as a means of representation rather, children perform actions as a means to master language and symbolic thought. Socio dramatic play, in which children play with others and create elaborate plots and characters, culminate in the understanding of representational thought and activity. However, children in this stage still struggle to understand dual representation– the idea that an object can be *both* an object and a symbol. Much thought during the preoperational phase is also egocentric – focused only on the child's point of view. During the concrete operational phase, a major turning point in cognition occurs the appearance of more logical and organized thought. Several key thinking processes emerge during this phase-*reversibility, seriation, and transitive inference.* Reversibility is the capacity to go through a series of steps and mentally reverse them, ending up back at the beginning. Seriation is the ability to order items by a quantitative dimension, such as height or weight. Transitive inference is a relational concept in which children can understand how objects related to one another. In terms of behavior during the concrete operational stage, children develop more capacity for learning, and most are excited to learn new things by undergoing formal schooling. In fact, the school experience seems to enhance the stages of Piaget's cognitive developmental theory.[20]

Children's Pretend Play and Thinking

As teachers and parents know, pre-school children engage

in a lot of pretend play, at least in middle-class modern societies. Yet even though play often has a distinctly social flavor, it seems to build distinctly *cognitive* skills, and may thus constitute a bridge between the social world and the more individualistic world of cognitive skills. For this purpose, play involving pretense is especially important for cognition. Pretense affects thinking in three ways: by its effect on reading others' intentions, by its encouragement of social referencing, and by its requirement of distinguishing between the real and the imaginary.

Learning as Development and Development as Learning

Although this chapter has obviously not covered all possible developmental changes about cognition, it has shown some important, direct ways that cognitive development relates to early childhood education and vice versa. The two areas emphasized – play and literacy – constitutes priorities for most early childhood programs. Each area gets underway or begins developing only if certain representational and classification abilities have already become established. Yet play and literacy also *contribute* to these cognitive abilities, taking them to new levels of richness and reflectivity. With time and practice, a child becomes aware of his or her own play, and of how language is used and intended, whether orally or in print. The resulting thoughtfulness allows for greater sophistication not only in play and literacy, but also in the related areas of social relationships and self-directed learning. For an early childhood teacher to provide opportunities for play and literacy, then, is to facilitate a bootstrapping of learning by development and of development by learning.

Theories of development are much more specific than paradigms or worldviews (Miller, 1993). A theory of development deals with change over time and is usually concerned with three things.

Numerous theories of development have influenced educational practices during the 20th century (Aldridge, Kuby, & Strevy, 1992), and currently a shift is affecting theories of child development and education. Some of the historical and current theories that have influenced education include Gesell's (1925) maturational theory, Skinner's (1974) behaviorist approach, Freud's (1935) psychoanalytic theory, Piaget's (1952) constructivist theory, Vygotsky's (1978) socio historical approach, Bron fenbrenner's (1989) ecological systems theory, and Gardner's (1983) multiple intelligences theory. has influenced education and child development practices, even though critical theory is not a theory of development.

Maturational Theory

The maturational theory of Arnold Gesell (1925) continues to affect what goes on in schools, particularly in early childhood classrooms in some parts of the United States. Gesell based his theory on three major assumptions:

(a) development has a biological basis,

(b) good and bad years alternate, and

(c) body types (endomorph, ectomorph, and mesomorph) are correlated with personality development (Thomas, 1992).

Maturational theory strongly influenced the teaching of reading in the mid 1900s (Morphett & Washburne, 1931). Children were not thought to be ripe for reading until they had a mental age of six and a half years. Consequently, readiness activities were developed for children who were not yet ready to read. Today, maturational theory is partially responsible for the existence of prekindergarten and pre first grades aimed at children who supposedly need the "gift of time," because of immaturity or a late birthday. These class rooms tend to have a ratio of boys to girls of any where from 7:1 to 10:1.

Practitioners subscribing to maturational theory consider any difficulties a child experiences as being found *within* the child. This over simplistic explanation for anything from reading problems to Attention Deficit (Hyperactivity) Disorder is extremely limiting to children and to those who work with them. If a problem lies within a child, then what value does a supportive (or, for that matter, a non supportive) environment have? Another, perhaps unintentional consequence of maturational theory is the recently popular "late birthday" phenomenon. Children in class rooms who are the youngest and have a "late birthday" are often branded by the teacher as slower and less ready for instruction.

BEHAVIORIST THEORY OF CHILDHOOD EDUCATION

Basics of the Theory

Famous psychologist B.F. Skinner's model, known as operant conditioning, centered on learned behaviors with an emphasis on the idea that satisfying or reinforced behaviors are conditioned responses, but punished behaviors can become eliminated and replaced with desirable ones. By this model, a student who receives oral praise or privileges for completing work quietly will continue to do so, while a student who talks out of turn and gets a reprimand or punishment will cease to talk without permission. The educator removes something positive or adds something negative as an immediate and specific consequence of the child's behavior.[21]

Simple Applications

Teachers employ behaviorism most directly by praising and scolding students for their actions. A child who talks out, hits or cuts in line will be rebuked while a child whose behavior is more compliant will be encouraged and singled out for positive feedback. Educators place a gold star on papers that were completed correctly and neatly, while stickers are withheld from sloppy papers and those with bad grades. Noisy, impatient pupils have to wait while their quieter peers get to go first at games and fun projects. These basic classroom management techniques are designed to reinforce desired behaviors by example and eliminate negative choices.

Under the umbrella of a behaviorist educational approach, the teacher lays out a specific set of good and bad consequences for the students in relation to the classroom rules. Each negative consequence is designed to be immediate and commensurate to the offense.

Token Economy

In primary class rooms, students often get points, plastic coins or photocopied "dollars" for good behavior. In turn, bad behavior costs them tokens. Students accumulate these tokens over a prescribed period (a week, a month) and cash them in for prizes like candy or small toys from a prize box or treasure chest. This behaviorist practice ascribes a tangible monetary value to pro social behaviors to encourage students to discard undesirable practices in favor of reinforced overt actions. The Positive Behavior Interventions and Supports movement is rooted in behaviorism and acts as a school wide framework to reward pro social actions with a token economy.

John Bowlby

John Bowlby examined the attachment relationship between parents and their children. He identified four phases in which attachment develops. He believed that children are born with a variety of behaviors that encourage parents and others to be near to them. These proximity-seeking behaviors include laughing, gurgling and crying.

Quality in Early Childhood Teacher Education Programs

Although there is agreement that early childhood teacher professional development (both pre service and in service) should be of high quality, the nature of that quality has not been consistently defined. Researchers have recently made efforts to articulate quality criteria for professional development that occurs in settings beyond the higher education system (e.g., Tout, Zaslow, & Berry, 2005; Winton, Mc Collum, & Catlett, 2007; Zaslow & Martinez-Beck, 2005). Frequently, high quality is described;

(1) in terms of teacher behaviors that are correlated with a positive impact on children's development and learning (e.g., when

teachers provide specific and engaging feedback to children, children show improved social competence) (Wilson, Pianta, & Stuhlman, 2007) or;

(2) when such information is available, in terms of direct benefits to young children and their families.

Within the higher education system of teacher preparation, there has been a move away from so-called "input-based" criteria for quality (such as hours of "seat time" or course credits in specific content), toward output- or results-based criteria, such as knowledge or skills demonstrated by graduating students. The accreditation system led by the National Council for the Accreditation of Teacher Education (NCATE) has been influential in shaping this trend.[22]

Standards provide one approach to defining and assessing quality in early childhood teacher preparation. The National Association for the Education of Young Children (NAEYC) standards for early childhood professional preparation (Hyson, 2003; Hyson & Biggar, 2005; NAEYC, 2001) is the only national standards for programs that prepare early childhood educators. In effect, these standards define high-quality professional preparation in terms of sets of competencies that well-prepared graduates should possess. As defined in the five NAEYC standards and detailed in their key elements, high-quality programs produce students who have knowledge, skills, and professional dispositions within each of five areas:

Standard-1: knowing how young children develop and learn (e.g., being able to create environments in which all children thrive);

Standard-2: building family and community relationships (e.g., developing respectful, reciprocal relationships with families);

Standard 3: using assessment responsibly (e.g., knowing about observation and documentation);

Standard 4: teaching to promote children's learning (e.g., making evidence-based decisions about curriculum, using a range of appropriate, effective teaching practices, having essential content knowledge in areas such as literacy and math); and

Standard 5: becoming a professional in the early childhood field (e.g., being able to advocate for children, using ethical guidelines.[23]

These five standards and their key elements were developed in 2001, building on but substantially revising earlier versions. Consistent with discussions of "evidence-based practice" (Buysse & Wesley, 2006), the 2001 revision incorporated recent evidence about the characteristics of effective early childhood educators, drawn from research and from professional expertise and values.

Quality and Improvement in ECCE Teacher Education Programs

Whatever the current status of early childhood teacher education programs, the potential for improvement is always present, with the goal of building the capacity of all programs to produce effective teachers of young children. The primary focus was on the "insider" perspectives of those faculty and administrators who are responsible for maintaining and improving program quality.

Significance of Play

As per the findings of many research and Child development experts also agree that play is very important in the learning and emotional development of all children. Play helps children learn relationship and social skills, and develop values and ethics. Play should always be considered an essential part of a child's early education. It is multi-faceted. Although it should be a fun experience for the child, often many skills can be learned through play. Playing games that have a definite structure or rules do not become dominant until children start to enter elementary school. Board games, simple card games, ball games or skipping games that have specific rules will teach children cooperation, mutual understanding, and logical thinking. A playground can be a turned into a learning experience for a child. Although a playground traditionally has certain elements, these elements may pose an unsafe surrounding for the child.

TYPES OF PLAY

Functional play: Functional play helps children to develop motor and practice skills. This kind of play is normally done with toys or objects that are stackable, can be filled with water or sand or playing outdoors.

Water play: Water play or, sand play is a favorite amongst pre-school children and a valuable teaching tool for the children.

Constructive play: Constructive play is characterized by building or creating something. Toys that encourage this type of play are simple puzzles, building blocks, easy craft activities, and puppets. Generally a 4 or 5 year old children enjoy this type of play, but it continues to be enjoyable into the first and second grades of school.

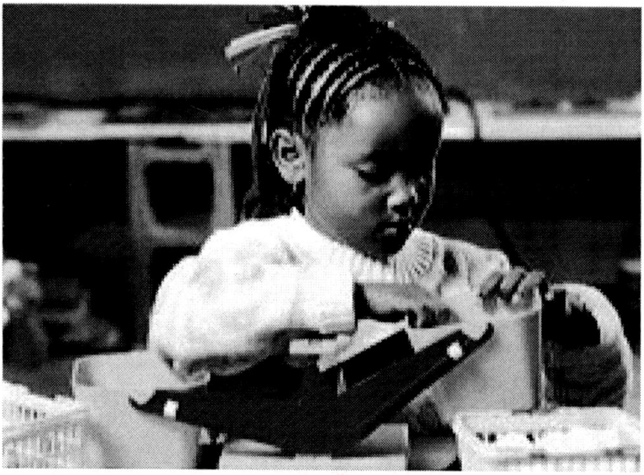

Hands and fingers are the best first art tools. Soon they will manage thick paint brushes, wedges of sponge etc. It is advised to avoid rushing a child into making something in particular. Letting

them do what they want encourages individuality and decision making. This type of play develops thinking and reasoning skills, problem solving, and creativity among the children.

Pretend play: Pretend play allows the children to express themselves and events in their lives. Pretend play helps children process emotions and events in their lives, practice social skills, learn values, develop language skills, and develop a rich imagination. This type of play is popular with children in preschool and kindergarten and it tends to fade out as they enter primary school.

Generally a child will transform themselves or a play object into someone or something else. Because of the important skills that are developed through this type of play, efforts should be made to encourage children to pretend.

A safe environment that allows gross motor activity is important for children. The following elements have been found to be unsafe in group care settings:

Metal slides can cause burns when the children are exposed to direct sunlight. The intense sunlight in a tropical climate heats metal to very high temperatures.

Traditional seesaws can result in injuries when one child unexpectedly jumps off.

Spring mounted, rocking toys with very heavy animal seats can strike a child. (There are acceptable, lighter weight rocking toy alternatives.)

Swings, other than tire swings, can easy hit a waiting child and cause injury. Light weight plastic seat swings pose a much lower chance hurting a child.

Things for Pre-school Curriculum

It is important that when considering an early education facility, caregivers and teacher in the facility have knowledge of the cultural supports for the language and literacy learning of the

children and families they are serving. They need to have sufficient skills in guiding small groups of children in order to give full attention to individual young children's language and literacy efforts. They need to be able to draw out shy children while they help very talkative ones begin to listen to others as well as to speak. Caregivers or teachers need to arrange environments that are symbol rich and interesting without being overwhelming to infants and toddlers. Even the simplest exchange becomes a literacy lesson when it includes the warmth of a relationship coupled with words, their concepts, and perhaps a graphic symbol.

To be effective, an early year's curriculum needs to be carefully structured. In that structure, there should be three strands: provision for the different starting points from which children develop their learning, building on what they can already do; relevant and appropriate content which matches the different levels of young children's needs; and planned and purposeful activity which provides opportunities for teaching and learning both indoors and outdoors.

If your child is between the ages of three and six and attends a pre-school or kindergarten program, the National Association for the Education of Young Children (NAEYC) suggests you look for these 10 signs to make sure your child is in a good class room:

1. Children spend most of their time playing and working with materials or other children. They do not wander aimlessly and they are not expected to sit quietly for long periods of time.
2. Children have access to various activities throughout the day. Look for assorted building blocks and other construction materials, props for pretend play, picture books, paints and other art materials, and table toys such as matching games, pegboards, and puzzles. All the children should not necessarily all be doing the same activity at the same time.
3. Teachers work with individual children, small groups, and the whole group at different times during the day. They do not spend all their time with the whole group.

4. The classroom is decorated with children's original art work, their own writing with invented spelling, and stories dictated by children to teachers.
5. Children learn numbers and the alphabet in the context of their everyday experiences. The natural world of plants and animals and meaningful activities like cooking, taking attendance or serving snack provides the basis for learning activities.
6. Children work on projects and have long periods of time (at least one hour) to play and explore. Work sheets are used little, if at all.
7. Children have an opportunity to play outside every day. Outdoor play is never sacrificed for more instructional time.
8. Teachers read books to children individually or in small groups throughout the day, not just at group story time.
9. Curriculum is adapted for those who are ahead as well as those who need additional help. Teachers recognize that children's different backgrounds and experiences mean that they do not learn the same things at the same time in the same way.
10. Children and their parents look forward to school. Parents feel secure about sending their child to the program. Children are happy to attend; they do not cry regularly or complain of feeling sick.

Pre-school Programs

Traditionally, pre-school programs were designed for children between the ages of 3 and 5 as a way to enhance social and emotional development. These nursery school options became popular in the 1920s and continue to be highly valued by many middle-class families. More recently, prekindergarten programs have been promoted as a way to help children identified as at-risk of failing in the K–12 system develop the skills they will need to be successful in later years. Many preschool programs today have also expanded their age range downward to include 2-year-olds rather than being full-day programs, most preschool classrooms operate half-time or less. A common model is to enroll children for three to five half-day sessions per week. With the increasing numbers of single parents and dual-career families, however, these partial-day sessions are often combined with the chance for children to participate in full-day child care as well. Pre-school students may be in the same class rooms and working with the same adults as students in child-care options, thus making it difficult to separate the two programs.[24]

The quality of any education programme can only be as good as the teacher who teaches it; how good and competent the teacher is, depends in turn, on how she has been prepared for her role as a teacher. The National Curriculum Framework for Teacher Education (NCFTE), 2009 acknowledges this to be a key factor and articulates the concern that "generally those who function as teacher educators do not possess appropriate stage specific professional training or experience" and this lacuna percolates down the system.

This becomes particularly relevant in the context of the early childhood stage which comprises of the first six years of life and is of critical significance as the formative stage of education and of a child's life. There is plentiful national and international empirical evidence to corroborate that the nature of care and education provided in the early years has implications for all subsequent stages of the education ladder. Moreover, it has its distinct stage specific characteristics and is required to be informed more by insights from child development and child psychology rather than skills-based academic priorities. To quote the NCFTE (2009) again, "Early Childhood Care and Education (ECCE) aims at total child development in a learning environment that is joyful, child centered, play and activity based. These requirements call for a teacher educator who has a sound educational philosophy of ECCE besides specialized content and methodology skills pertaining to these areas."

A key question therefore is – do the teacher education programs being currently offered in India enable the required expertise and experience and prepare student teachers adequately for the demands of this critical stage of children's development and their education? Being an unregulated sector, there is to date very little documented information available in this area to answer this query appropriately.

Growing Significance of ECCE

Awareness, knowledge and practices that address the psychological, social, physical and well being needs of young children below 6 years continue to evolve across the world, slowly and sometimes in disparate ways. A significant body of research and writing in ECCE has emerged in the last few decades. Worldwide, many early childhood programmes continue to work with conventional beliefs about how young children grow, think, learn and interact. Unregulated early schooling practices continue to exist despite UN ratified rights-based perspectives in early childhood education that lay emphasis on the need for equitable opportunities, play, emotional care, nurturing social interaction, and experiential learning. Young children who live in high risk situations because of poverty, social neglect and other factors.

Preparing teachers for Early Childhood Care and Education violent or war-like situations particularly bear the brunt of the amorphously defined structures and processes of the field of ECCE. Till only a few decades ago, most societies believed that young children from birth till as 6 years of age tend to be passive recipients of learning and socialization. Research based insights about early childhood development after the second world war, led by M. Mahler, B. Bowlby, Maria Montessori, Froebel, John Dewey, Piaget and L. Vygostky and more recently Daniel Stern et. al., helped relocate the agency of the very young child as an active participant in his/her process of growing up. Recently, a range of research studies on the early development of the human brain have reinstated the works of these thinkers and established new ground about how children learn and interact in their daily lives. Studies have not only re-established the significance of nutrition and early cognitive stimulation but also make overt connections between the emotional nurturance of young children and their brain development.[25]

New brain research has clearly established that the human brain grows at a rapid pace after birth and reaches 85 per cent of its adult weight by the time the child is 2 years old; it then continues on an incline till around six years of life, beyond which it tends to plateau. Within this span of six years several 'critical periods' have been identified for development of some important cognitive, linguistic and social competencies, which if subjected to psycho-social deprivation, can adversely impact on development of children's full potential. (Doherty, 1997). Research based insight thus confirms the significance of the first six years of life. Research also establishes that the environment in which a child is raised directly impacts the way the brain develops. Logically, insights from research in ECCE and Neuroscience have major implications for how we organize care, stimulation and education of young children at home and in institutions.

Empirical evidence is also available from around the world of the significant impact, both immediate and long term, of participation in ECCE on the life trajectory of young children. A longitudinal study of the impact of ECCE from Chicago (conducted between 1986 and 2002) revealed that children who attended state supported early childhood intervention centres demonstrated better results in language and mathematics learning in school, achieved higher rates of high school completion, were less likely to be placed in special education and had lower rates of juvenile arrest Studies conducted by National Council of Educational Research and Training (NCERT) and National Institute of Public Cooperation and Child Development (NIPCCD) in India in the 1990s have also documented benefits of participation in ECCE programmes on primary level outcomes. A study across eight states of the country followed up on 38000 children and demonstrated an increase in retention rates by as much as 20.5 per cent because of participation in ECCE programmes (Kaul et. al, 1994). Clearly, it establishes the contribution of ECCE in the success rates of children in school in later years.

Consequently, ECCE has been globally identified as the first goal to be reached under UNESCO's Education For All (EFA) initiative, to which India is a signatory. Unfortunately, despite this acknowledgement of the importance of the relationship between the quality of early learning and care available for young children and their adaptability in later life and society, wide gaps continue to exist in the way societies prepare young children for formal schooling, and for life.

In developing countries, owing to challenging economic and political conditions, early care has largely been about allocating resources for the physical survival of young children, primarily immunization and nutrition. The history of the development of early childhood care and education as a practice, as a field of enquiry, of professional development and research has received inconsistent support in terms of policy, funds allocation and prioritization. At the same time, preparation of early childhood practitioners and professionals has also not been commensurate with burgeoning socio-economic and political complexities. While institutional training and preparation has evolved very slowly, demands for the care and education of young children have progressed far too rapidly, particularly with the disruption of the joint family system and with more and more women joining the work force. The context of Early Childhood Care and Education in India with a population of over a billion people, India has more than 350 million children between 0 and 18 years of age. Of these, about 157.86 million are between 0 and 6 years of age.[26]

ECCE in International Framework: A Contextual Analysis

ECCE has vast potential for human development. This was first highlighted in article 25(2) of the Universal Declaration of Human Rights, 1948 that recognizes that childhood is entitled to special care and assistance. The concern for childcare and education was further culminated in the United Nations Convention on the Rights of the Child, 1989. The Convention focuses on the whole gamut of human rights necessary for a child to develop his/her potential. The Convention sets global standards for ensuring child rights to Survival, Protection, Development, and Participation as per the legal systems and cultural traditions of the respective State Parties. Following the CRC, rounds of conferences have been held at the international level to advance the goal of Education for All (EFA) with the objective to ensure 'Right to Education' as a basic "Human Right." The Jometin Declaration, 1990 and Darkar Framework for Action, 2000 were drawn on the Universal Declaration of Human Rights, 1948, and CRC, 1989. Let us brief the international frameworks where the subject of ECCE is either implied or overt.

United Nations Declaration of the Rights of the Child, 1959

In 1959, United Nations came out with the Declaration of the Rights of the Child. The spirit of the Declaration was reflected in the preamble, which said, "Mankind owes to the child the best it has to give". The Declaration affirms the rights of the child to enjoy special protection and facilities to develop in a healthy and normal manner in conditions of freedom and dignity, to have name and nationality, social security, adequate nutrition, medical services, to grow up in an atmosphere of affection, to receive education, protection from exploitation and finally the right of the child to be brought up "in a spirit of understanding, tolerance, friendship among peoples, peace and universal brotherhood".

United Nations' Convention on the Rights of the Child (UNCRC), 1989

The adoption of Convention on the Rights of the Child (CRC) by the United Nations General Assembly on November 20, 1989 was a revelation in the history of international child rights movement. The recognition of early childhood rights in the United Nations Convention on the Rights of the Child (1989) is reflected in its preamble, speaking "the child, by reason of his physical and mental immaturity, need special safeguards and care, including appropriate legal protection, before as well as after birth". The underlying philosophy of the Convention got proximity for action by requiring the State Parties to recognize the inherent right to life of every child and to ensure to the maximum extent possible the survival and development of the child. State Parties are required to render appropriate assistance to parents and legal guardians in the performance of their child-rearing responsibilities and to ensure the development of institutions, facilities and services for the care of children.

The Convention also mandates the State Parties to take appropriate measures for the children of working parents to have right to benefit from child-care services and facilities.The Convention, of course, is the first legally binding international instrument to focus on the whole spectrum of human rights–civil and political rights as well as economic, social and cultural rights - necessary for a child for realization of fullest development. Direct or indirect reference to ECCE is made in the following provisions of CRC:

(i) Right against discrimination on the ground of child's or his or her parent's or legal guardian's race, colour, sex , language, religion, political or other opinion, national, ethnic or social origin, property, disability ,birth or other status (Article-2.1);

(ii) Responsibility of State to ensure the child such care as is necessary for his/her well-being. (Article3.2);

(iii) State Party respect to the responsibilities, rights and duties of parents or family or community as regards to local customs (Article-5);

(iv) Right to life (Article-6.1);

(v) Right to survival and development (Article-6.2);

(vi) Right to Birth Registration and Right to a name , nationality and parenthood (Article-7.1);

(vii) Obligation of State to render appropriate assistance to parents/ guardians in the performance of child rearing responsibility (Article -18.2);

(viii) Children of working parents shall have rights to benefit from the child care services (Artivle-18.3);

(ix) Special protection and assistance to child who is deprived of his or her family environment. Aricle-20);

(x) Right to special care for children with disabilities (Article-23);

(xi) Right to highest attainable standards of health and health care facilities (Article-24.1);

(xii) State Party obligation to diminish infant and child mortality, to combat disease and malnutrition , to provide adequate nutritious foods and clean drinking water, to ensure appropriate pre-natal and prost-natal health care for mothers, to promote advantages of barest feeding and to take effective appropriate measures for abolishing traditional practices pre-judicial to the health of the children (Aricle-24.2 and 3);

(xiii) Right to adequate standard of living for physical, metal, spiritual, moral, and social development (Article-27.1);

(xiv) State Party obligation to provide education ensuring development of child personality, talent and mental and physical abilities to the fullest potential (Article-29).[27]

The Convention confers wide range of rights to the young children and these rights broadly revolve around the survival, protection and development of children. Succinctly put, the UNCRC endows the following rights to the young children–

- Right to born free and Right to Life.
- Right to Breast-Feeding.
- Right to Birth Registration.
- Right to Food.
- Right to Health.
- Right to Parental/ Family Care.
- Right to Institutional Care.
- Right against Abandonment.
- Right to Early Childhood Education.
- Right to avail Benefit from Social Security Programmes.

United Nations not only set international guidelines for child rights or set target for the State Parties, but programmes concerning to children are either monitored or funded or organized by the United Nations Body and International Organizations. The progress made by the State Parties in realization of underlying CRC provisions in the domestic sphere is reviewed by a Committee in every five years interval following to the Initial Report, which needs to be submitted within the two years of State Party ratification to this Convention. The Convention requires the involvement of United Nations Organs or Specialized Agencies like UNICEF for the implementation of the provisions of CRC. UNICEF is required to submit reports to the UN Committee on the implementation of the Convention in areas falling within the scope of its activities. As the UNICEF is directly or indirectly involved with process of achieving the Millennium Development Goals in the respective State Party area, it regularly monitors the progress and submits Progress Report to the United Nations Committee.

The CRC, due its extent across countries and breadth of rights under its ambit, constitutes a landmark international commitment towards child rights. It reaffirms the right to free and compulsory primary schooling without any type of discrimination. The UNCRC asserts the right of every child to education, without discrimination, and places particular emphasis on making primary education compulsory and available free to all (Article-28).

In 2005, The UN Committee on the Rights of the Child had gone a step further by interpreting every child's right to education as beginning at birth and closely tied to right to development, as spelt out in Article-6.2 of the UNCRC. The Committee also recommends that States Parties shall pay greater attention to, and actively support, a right-based approach to early childhood programs.

UNESCO World Declaration on Education for All

UNESCO adopts a holistic approach to ECCE in order ensure the right to education for all. World Education Conferences have been held where National Governments and International Organizations have reaffirmed and renewed their commitments for making Education for All a reality. Global quest to universalize primary education had marked the beginning from the World Conference on EFA, which was held at Jometin, Thailand (5-9 March, 1990). It broadened the scope of education by recognizing that 'learning begins at birth' (Article-V), and 'learning does not take place in isolation... all learners should receive nutrition, health care, physical and emotional support' (Article-VI). It called for the provision for early childhood care and initial education though arrangements involving families, communities, or institutional programmes.

A decade later, the World Education Forum was held at Darkar, Senegal on 26-28 April 2000. That was the most important international education conference where 1,100 participants including 164 country governments together with representatives of regional groups, international organizations, non-government organizations, civil society reaffirmed their commitment to achieving Education For All by the year 2015 and entrusted UNESCO with the overall responsibility of co-coordinating all international players and sustaining global momentum. The Darkar Framework for Action (DFA) renewed the importance of early childhood and included the development of ECCE as the first of its six main goals. The representatives at the World Education Forum pledged themselves to achieve, "expanding and improving comprehensive early childhood care and education, especially for the vulnerable and disadvantaged children."[28]

UNO's Millennium Development Declarations, 2000

The Millennium Summit was held from 6-8 September 2000 where Member States of the United Nations ratified the Millennium Development Declarations of which Millennium Development Goals (MDGs) was a part.[29] The MDGs have 8 international development goals with 21 targets to which 192 Member States of the UN and 23 International Organizations are agreed to achieve by the year 2015.One of the goals was to achieve universal primary education with a target that by 2015, children everywhere, boys and girls, would be able to complete a full course of primary schoolings.

Undeniably, the most important proposition to ensure right to education is developing school readiness among the children. This could be possible only by providing opportunity for children to have access to quality early childhood education service. Integrated Child Development Services (ICDS) scheme is a flagship programme in India which offers pre-school education along-with supplementary nutrition, immunization, health check-up and referral services to under-6 years aged children. Whereas Section-11 of the Right of Children to Free and Compulsory Education Act, 2009 puts a legal obligation on State to make necessary arrangements for providing free pre-school education to children above the age of 3 years.

SPECIAL INITIATIVES

National Charter for Children (2004)

The Charter is intended to secure the inherent rights of children for survival and development. This also aims to address the root causes that negate growth and development of children.

Commission for Protection of Child Rights Act (2005)

The Act creates National Commission at the National level and the State Commissions at the State level.The Commissions would be working for proper enforcement of children's rights and effective implementation of laws and promgrammes relating to children.

Integrated Child Protection Scheme

This Scheme proposes to provide institutional as well as non-institutional support for children living under difficult circumstances in order to provide immediate care and protection as well as long term rehabilitations to them.

Integrated Scheme for Street Children

The objective of this scheme is to prevent destitution of children and facilitate their withdrawal from life on the streets. The programme provides for basic facilities to street children and seeks to protect them against abuse and exploitation.

References

1. Byrne, B. (1998). The foundation of literacy: the child's acquisition of the alphabetic principle. Hove, East Sussex, UK: Psychology Press.
2. A Study for Urban childhood programmes by Dr. Vrinda datta, Tata Institute of Social Sciences.
3. Bissex, G. (1980). Gnys at work: A child learns to write and read. Cambridge, MA: Harvard University Press.
4. Bredekamp, S. & Copple, C. (eds.). (1997). Developmentally appropriate practice in early childhood programs: revised edition. Washington, D.C.: National Association for the Education of Young Children.
5. Gelman, R. & Baillargeon, R. (1998). A review of some Piagetian concepts. In P. Mussen, J. Flavell & E. Markman (Eds.), Handbook of Child Psychology, Volume 3: Cognitive Development. New York: Wiley.
6. My name is today-Children in News, Rights of the Child, BUCCERFLIES, New Delhi.
7. National consultation on ECCD, issues and challenges for advocacy, Forces, New Delhi.
8. National Plan of Action for Children (1992).
9. National Policy for Children (1974).
10. National Policy for Education (1986)
11. Planning effective for Pre–School education, Centre for health education training and nutrition (CHETNA).
12. Playing to learn: training for Early childhood education by Mina Swaminathan Foundation Madras.

Notes

1. http://en.wikipedia.org/wiki/Early_childhood_education
2. Early Childhood Care And Education, by M. Sen Gupta, PHI Learning Pvt. Ltd., 2009.
3. Early Childhood Care and Education and Equality of Opportunity-Burger, Kaspar, 2013, IX, 235 p.
4. TP Krogh. S. L. & Slentz. K. L. (2001); Early Childhood Education: yesterday, today & tomorrow; Mahwah, New Jersey: Lawrence Erlbaum Associates, Inc.
5. TP Bredekamp, S. (Ed). (1987). Developmentally appropriate practice in early childhood programmes serving children from birth through age 8, Washington, DC: National Association for the Education of Young Children.
6. Schweinhart, L. J. & Weikart, D. P. (March, 1998). Why Curriculum Matters in Early Childhood Education. Educational Leadership. 57-60.
7. Frede, E, & Barnett, W. S. (1992). Developmentally Appropriate public school Preschool: A study of implementation of the High/Scope curriculum and its effects on Disadvantaged children's skills at first grade. Early Childhood Research Quarterly, 7(4), 483-499.
8. Marcon, R. (Spring, 2002). Moving up the grades: Relationship between preschool model and later school success. Early Childhood Research and Practicehttp://ecrp.uiuc.edu/v4n1/marcon.html
9. Barnett, S. W. (1995). Long-term effects of early childhood programmes on cognitive and school outcomes, The Future of Children, 5(3), 25-50. www.futureofchildren.org
10. Barbara Ruth Peltzman; "Pioneers of Early Childhood Education: A Pro-Bibliographical Guide"(1998) GreenWood Press, Westport CT Publication London.
11. John Locke (1632-1704), an English philosopher, set out the principles of empiricism. He advanced the hypothesis that people learn primarily from external forces. Locke examined how people acquire ideas in An Essay Concerning Human Understanding (1690).

12. Rousseau's Émile: Or, Treatise on Education, Author-Jean-Jacques Rousseau, Translated by William Harold Payne, - D. Appleton, 1909, Original from University of Minnesota, Volume 20 of International education seriesVolume 20 of International education series: D. Appleton.
13. Dewey, J. (1986b). The need for a philosophy of education. In J. A. Boydston (ed.), John Dewey: The later works, 1925–1953, Vol. 9 (pp. 194–204). Carbondale: Southern University Press. (original work published 1934).
14. http://www.scholastic.com/teachers/article/pioneers-our-field-jean-piaget-champion-childrens-ideas.
15. History of Early Childhood Education Maria Montessori (1870-1952) United States Department of Education www.ed.gov
16. Theories of Child Development: National Association for the Education of Young Children www.naeyc.org. National for Early Development and Learning www.fpg.unc.edu/~ncedl/ Center. No Child Left Behind www.nochildleftbehind.gov. United States Department of Education www.ed.gov
17. Social Constructivist : Theory and Principles of Inclusion: Challenges for Early Childhood Special Education by Bruce L. Mallory, University of New Hampshire and Rebecca S. New, University of New Hampshire.
18. Vygotsky, L. S. (1962). Thought and language. Cambridge, MA: MIT Press and Wiley and http://www.education.com/reference/article/vygotsky-lev-semenovich-1896-1934.
19. Kelvin L. Seifert, University of Manitoba.
20. https://www.boundless.com/psychology/human development/infancy-and-childhood/cognitive-development-in-childhood/
21. Lora Mathews, Demand Mediahttp://everydaylife.globalpost.com/behaviorist-theory-childhood-education-3963.html
22. http://www.ncate.org
23. http://www.naeyc.org/faculty/standards.asp
24. Expat Web Site Association Jakarta, Indonesia http://www.expat.or.id

25. Sources: http://www.nea.org
26. (http://www.sccommissioners.org/ pdfs/primers/icdsguidelines.
27. UNCRC, United Nations Convention on the Rights of the Child, 1989, Nov.20.
28. UNESCO; EFA Global Monitoring Report, 2008.
29. www.un.org/millennium/declaration/ares552e.html

6

Early Childhood Care and Education in Odisha

Profile of Odisha State

Odisha is one of the major states of the union of India, was created on 01 April in the year 1936. It has an area of 155,707 square kilometers, which constitutes 4.74 percent of the total geographical area of India. There are 3 revenue divisions, 30 districts, 58 sub-divisions, and 171 tehasils, 314 community development blocks, 6234 Gram-panchayatas, 103 urban local bodies and 51,349 villages in the State. The State Odisha extends from 17° 49'N to 22° 34'N latitude and from 81° 29'E to 87° 29'E longitude on the eastern coast of India. Odisha has a population of more than 36.8 million as per census-2011, accounting for 7.58 percent of India's population. The decadal population growth rate was 19.9 percent against Country's growth rate of 21.5 between 2001-2011. 0 to 6 years aged child population of the State was 9.4 million, precisely constituted 19.6 percent of the State total population. Among the 0-6 year aged child population, the ST children accounted 26.7 percent and SC shared 17.5 percent. The sex ratio among aggregate population is 972 and sex ratio for children (0-6 year) is 952.

Odisha is the homeland of 62-schedule tribe communities of them 13 tribes have been declared as primitive tribes. Schedule Tribes constitute 23.0 percent of State's total population. Nearly 16.5 percent of the State population belongs to the Schedule Castes. The overall literacy rate, as per Census-2011, is more than 63.08%

with 59.8 per cent in rural and 80.8 per cent in urban Odisha. The literacy rate of Schedule Tribe and Schedule Caste population has been much lower than rest of the population. As against the overall literacy rate of 63.08 per cent in the State, the literacy rate of 43.3 per cent among the Schedule Tribes is considerably below. The schedule tribe female literacy rate of 29.1 per cent is much lower than the State average female literacy of 50.5 per cent. Around 40 per cent of State's population is below the poverty line.[1]

Tribal Context in Odisha

Odisha is one of the poorer states in India located on the east coast of India with an estimated population of about 40 million in 2010. The capital of Odisha is Bhubaneswar and Odiya is the official state language and most widely spoken but there also exist 23 tribal languages in the state. The indigenous people called *Adivasi* are classified as Scheduled Tribes and constitute 9.1 per cent of the Indian population (Census 2011). Odisha has the third largest concentration of tribal population in the country and combined with seven other states accounts for more than 80 per cent of the tribal population of India. The population of scheduled tribes of Odisha is 8,145,081, which is 9.7 per cent of the tribal population of the country and 22.1 per cent of the total population of the state. There are 62 tribal groups officially recognized in Odisha. The Scheduled Tribe population of the state is overwhelmingly rural with 94.5 per cent residing in villages.

The tribal communities are relatively isolated and thrive on subsistence-based economy relying heavily on forest produce, hunting, fishing, shifting cultivation and primitive agriculture. The percentage of households below the poverty line is the highest among the scheduled tribes as compared to other social groups. Gradually, they are adopting modern agricultural processes. Their aesthetic senses are manifested in the architectural designs of their settlements and house patterns, art and craft, personal belongings, materials of daily use made out of locally available resources, musical instruments, costumes, hunting weapons, fishing nets and traps, basketry and utensils and even in agricultural equipments. The tribal's of Odisha have got wide recognition for their folk tales, myths, dance and music and various types of performing art.

Special educational schemes have contributed to the educational progress of the scheduled castes and the scheduled tribes. However *Adivasis* continue to lag behind educationally. Many SC/ST parents are unable to send their children to 'free' schools because of costs other than the tuition fee and the cost of forgone income from children's work. The literacy rate of the people in the State has been calculated at 63 per cent while the rate in the tribal districts of the State is at 37.37 per cent.

The social distance of the tribal communities from the majority and high caste communities is very large. Teachers impose their own culture and value systems on tribal children, which is often alien to these communities. Tribal children often start school in a language that is not their mother tongue. Even the content of most books is alien to an Adivasi child and does not attract the tribal child as something relevant or interesting.

ICDS in Tribal Areas

Integrated Child Development Service, conceived in 1975, is the only major national programme that addresses the issue of under-six children. Although tribal people have distinct culture, language and separate identity, there is no special kind of child care services for the scheduled tribe children except the provision for one Anganwadi Center (AWC) for 700 populations in the tribal areas as against 1000 population in other areas. There are approximately 13 million under-6 scheduled tribe children. Looking at the economic deprivation and educational backwardness of tribal community, all the under-six scheduled tribe children need center based early childhood care and education services. The major services of ICDS are immunization, health check-up, supply of nutritious foods, pre-primary education- are directed to reduce infant mortality, reduce under-5 mortality, combat malnutrition, and to prepare child for school readiness.

ICDS services for tribal children are not adequate for at least two reasons. First, the number of AWCs are quite less than the requirements and even not par with the central norms fixed for the opening of AWC in the tribal areas. The existing norms permit one AWC per every 700 population in the tribal areas. Further, in hilly or desert areas, one AWC is permissible for a population of 300. There is also provision of one AWC in a population of 150-300 for remote and low populated hamlet villages in the tribal areas. According to an estimation of HAQ: Center for Child Rights, the requirements of AWCs in Scheduled Tribe dominated areas is 2, 02,276. Secondly, the services of ICDS, particularly pre-primary non formal education are not being imparted according to the culture and language of Tribal.

Situational Analysis: The children below the age of six years constitute one-seventh of the total population of Orissa. There are around 4.5 million 0-5 years aged child population in the State of which 2.56 million are 3-5 years aged (State Plan of Action for Children; 2009-12; Government of Odisha; W & CD Department). The State of young children in Orissa is found to be lagging behind in respect to health, nutrition, early childhood education, and primary education in comparison to national average.

Pre-School Education: Through ICDS, more than 14.4 lakh children are covered for pre-school education, which is estimated to be around 56 percent of total pre-school aged child population. According to Annual Status Education Report (Rural) 2008, 26.3 percent of 3 years aged and 20.9 percent of 4 years aged children are not attending pre-school education anywhere.

Primary Education: The Net Enrolment Rate and Completion Rate in primary classes (Class-I-V) are increased by 4.4 and 8.4 points respectively between 2011-13 to 2013-15:

- Transition rate from Primary to Upper Primary is increased from 76.35 percent in 2011-13 to 88.37 percent in 2013-15.
- The drop out in primary level (Class I-V) is 27.8 among all

category of children, 35.09 among scheduled caste, and 34.18 among schedule tribe children[3] belong to schedule tribe.

- The dropout rate among schedule tribe children is comparatively higher in primary as well as in elementary level.
- Out of every 100 children enrolled, only 18 of them complete education of Class-VIII.
- More than half (55.6) of total out of school children belong to schedule tribes·
- Tribal children have limited opportunity of access to pre-primary education.
- The difference between home language and school language is the major reasons for high dropout in the primary level.

Nutrition: The majority of children go through life in a state of nutritional deficiency. They are anemic, malnourished, and underweight.

- Two-Thirds of children of 6-59 months are anemic.

Among under-3 years aged children, 44.0 percent are stunted (Low Height for Age), 40.0 percent are underweight (Low Weight for Age), and 24.0 percent are wasted (Low for Height). The Government of Orissa has prepared the State Plan of Action for Children which sets out the proximate goals to improved the health, nutritional status and educational attainment of children, considering ECCE as a significant feeder and support to universal enrolment in school, the State Plan of Action proposes to ensure ECE to all in order to achieve 100 per retention in schools and to reduce dropouts.

Programme Implemented in Odisha for ECCE Service

Across the country, ICDS is the major programme in the state of Odisha that delivers services to children aged below six years for their holistic development. There are also provisions under SSA to provide early childhood care and education to children particularly in non-ICDS coverage area. The intervention of SSA is a strategy of experimentation of implementation of ECCE programme in ICDS non-coverage areas as well as strengthening the pre-school education service of ICDS by providing training to the AWWs and supplying pre-school education kits to AWCs. There are more than 3938 (1678 centers under SSA and 2260 centers under NREGEL) ECCE centers have been opened under SSA and NPEGEL to address the pre-school education issue of 3-5 years aged children. Irrespective of the policy approach of ECCE in SSA/NPEGEL, the ICDS is the flagship programme that addresses the issue childcare and early childhood education. By and large ICDS covers all the 314 blocks and 12 urban local bodies through the network of more than 60,918 Anganwadi and 10,216 Mini-Anganwadi Centers.

Landscape of ICDS Programme in Odisha

As a part of the national programme, ICDS was launched in Odisha 1975 in Sunabeda Block of Sundergarh district with 85 AWCs. Since then it has been extended to more than 326 Projects including all 314 Community Development Blocks, and 12 Urban Local Bodies. There are more than 71,134 Centers (60,918 Anganwadi+10,216 Mini-Anganwadi) were sanctioned, out which 41,697 numbers of centers which are in operation.

Kinds of Programme

The children below six years, pregnant women and lactating mothers are the beneficiaries of ICDS services. The scheme provides a comprehensive package of services to children that integrate supplementary nutrition with primary health care and informal education. The services provide to children through ICDS include, supplementary nutrition, immunization, health check-up, growth monitoring, pre-school non-formal education.

ECCE Accessibility

Supplementary feeding and pre-school education are the two most important components of ICDS scheme. Special focus is being given to the pre-school education component of ICDS scheme, so that the children are fully prepared for entering Class-I at the age of 6 years. Early Childhood Care and Education under ICDS is a crucial component that aims at universalisation and qualitative improvement of primary education. The early childhood/pre-school education programme, conducted through the non-formal and play-way method, aims at providing a learning environment for all-round development of the child (Annual Activity Report DWCD, Government of Odisha). The total child beneficiaries under SNP during 2008-09 were 41,10,460 out of which 40,74,342 were normal, and mild, and moderately malnourished children and 36,118 were severely malnourished children. In pre-school education programme, 18.4 lakh 3-6 year aged children were enrolled in 2010-11.

As per NFHS-3 Report, in Odisha 65.8 per cent of children aged below six years is received with any services of ICDS.[2] To further disaggregate, 62.5 per cent of children have received food supplements in the form of either cooked food or home rations, 51.6 per cent have received immunizations, 43.1 per cent have received health check-up. Only 37.7 per cent of pre-school aged children are going to the anganwadi centers for pre-school education. According to Annual Status of Education Report (Rural) - 2010, 26.3 per cent of 3 years aged children, and 20.9 per cent of 4 years aged children in the State are deprived of receiving ICDS service. Only 23.8 per cent of 5 years aged children have received pre-school education through ICDS.

Infrastructure Facilities

Out of the total of 60,918 sanctioned AWCs 15,952 centers have their own building; 10,287anganwadis are placed in school buildings; and 34,679 Anganwadis are operating in rented/ community house or somewhere else. The basic facilities in the anganwadis are unsatisfactory. It was revealed from evaluation study conducted by the National Institute of Nutrition that Anganwadis in Odisha do not have adequate building, and function in an unhygienic physical environment. Information obtained from the website[3] of DWCD of Government of Odisha reveals that, 36.6 per cent do not have drinking water facilities. 53.57 per cent anganwadis have sourced water from tube well, 4.44 per cent from well, 3.60 per cent from bore well, and 1.75 per cent anganwadis have piped water facilities, 7.2 per cent of Anganwadis do not have toilet facilities. Baby friendly toilets are available in 14.9 per cent centers, safety toilets in 4.9 per cent centers, and Barapali toilets in 1.7 per cent centers. Flush type of toilets is available in minuscule percentage of Anganwadi centers.

Under ICDS scheme, supplementary nutrition in the form of hot cooked nutrient foods is provided to children. It is necessary to prepare foods for which Anganwadi centers should have kitchens, cooking utensils, feeding utensils and storage facilities for keeping the food grains. But majority of the Anganwadis do not have these facilities. Kitchens are available in 29.7 per cent of centers, and 20.3 per cent of centers have feeding utensils. Even more than half of Anganwadis are equipped with cooking utensils, less than one-fifth of the total Anganwadis have both cooking and feeding utensils. Furniture such as chairs and tables are available in two-thirds of the Anganwadis whereas 10.6 per cent Anganwadis have alamirahs to keep records, learning, and game equipments.

Key Indicators of Young Children Status in Odisha

Odisha has highest percentage of Infant Deaths & Neo-Natal Deaths among the States of India. The IMR for the State is 83 per 1000 live births. The Neo-Natal Mortality is 61 per 1000 live births. 54.4 per cent Children born in Orissa are underweight. 20.7 per cent of children below 3 years of age are severely underweight and another 54.4 per cent are moderately underweight. Even after 40 years of its existence, ICDS still fail to reach every poor child. Services under ICDS covered only 2.5 million children in the age group of 0-6 years, while the children need early childhood care through ICDS network is estimated to be 4.0 Million. Adequate and appropriate infrastructure remains a major obstacle in the implementation of the programme. Although the enrolment at primary levels shows an increase in recent years, yet the level of retention in schools remain a matter of concern.

The enrolment ratio at upper primary level is not encouraging. The dropout rate is higher among girls, SC & ST children. It is an estimated that 336459 numbers of children are affected by serious physical or mental disabilities.[4] The Department of Women and Child Development was created for implementing different social welfare schemes meant for persons with disability, the old, infirm and indigent persons. Women & Child Development Department is committed for strengthening the initiatives of government for holistic development of women and child, which constitutes 49.3 per cent and 14.6 per cent of the Orissa's population. This is the Nodal Department for formulating plans and programmes for development of women and children in the State.

Mother-Tongue based Multi-lingual Early Childhood Education in Odisha

Odisha is home to more than 62 tribes including 13 particularly vulnerable tribal groups, who speak their own dialects which is different from mainstream Odiya. This, united with difficult geographical, demographic and socio cultural factors makes it difficult for children from tribal communities to learn main stream languages. Thus, when children from these tribal groups come into main stream schooling, learning becomes a challenge as they do not understand the language which is the medium of instruction.

The total population of Odisha is more than 4 crores out of which tribals constitute 22.13 per cent. The third largest concentration of tribal population in India lives in Odisha of the 8 million tribal people in the state 1.4 million are children between the ages of 0-6. Among this population, literacy rates are 37 per cent compared to 63 per cent for the state (65 per cent for the country) and primary school drop-out rates are 20 percentage points higher than the state average (24 points for tribal girls).

State of ECCE

Various Early Childhood Care and Development (ECCD) schemes under government and non-government agencies are able to reach out to only 19.6 percent of the 3-6 age group population. The United Nations Children's Fund (UNICEF) assisted Early Childhood Education (ECE) programme is being implemented in the state since 1982 with the objective of motivation children in the age group of 3-6 years toward primary education with a view to achieving the aim of UEE. Motivation of pre-school children is planned through use of basic learning and play materials developed by institutions set up under the ECCE programme. The ICDS projects and agencies like State Council of Child Welfare and State Social Welfare Advisory Board and administering. The pre-primary state education through Anganwadis. Balwadis and Creche centre. There has been a steady improvement in coverage under ICDS. The number of projects and Anganwadi Workers increased from time to time and Steps are being taken to extend the scheme.

As per the recent Global Monitoring Report, United Nations Educational, Scientific and Cultural Organisation (UNESCO), strong early childhood foundations including good health, nutrition and nurturing environment can ensure a smooth transition to primary schools, a better chance of completing elementary education and route to poverty and disadvantage.

Gaps and Inadequacies of Facilitators

To achieve the above objectives, a package of six integrated services is provided in a comprehensive manner to meet the multi-dimensional and interrelated needs of the children. The Anganwadi Centre forms the focal point for the delivery of these services.

Designed in 1975, both the original objectives of ICDS as well as the comprehensive package of six service offering care to the young child are extremely relevant. However, an evaluative review of ICDS programme has thrown up the number of gaps in the service delivery level which are discussed below.

First, ICDS programme does not have the balance linkage between health, nutrition and pre-primary education, ICDS is a programme of basic health (i.e., immunization, health check up) and supplementary feeding rather than a programme for early childhood education (i.e. pre-primary education). From policy approach to actual implementation, there are plenty of problems ICDS particular related to pre-school activities.

- Pre-school education at Anganwadi centers is hampered largely due to lack of basic infrastructure (i.e., building, space, play and game materials, learning kits),
- Untrained or inadequately trained pre-school instructor (AWW),
- Absence of standard pre-school curriculum indicating learning methods for pre-school activities, language to be used for communication;
- Lack of monitoring and supervision,
- Absence of community participation.

Apart from government initiatives, private sectors, corporate bodies, and missionaries are also providing early childhood education in the form of kindergarten, nursery or pre-school education in a variety of modes and varying degree of quality. The children of rich families and elite classes can afford to receive high quality early childhood education, whereas children of poor and unprivileged families are either deprived of getting early childhood education or integrated with the ICDS that renders poor quality service. Children from advantaged families tend to arrive at schools with higher level and school readiness, advanced cognitive skills, and positive approach to learning. Conversely, children entering into schools without pre-primary education have lower level of motivation, cognitive skills and are more often faced with difficulties to cope with the school systems. While the syllabi and curriculum adopted by Public School for pre-primary education have forward linkage with the primary education, ICDS sponsored pre-school education does not have such linkage.

Lastly, ICDS does not have any explicit programme to help

children prepare for school. By prepare for school, we do not refer to the of attempts made in some private institutions to advance the primary school curriculum or subject children to formal teaching methods, but to the gentle introduction of positive attitudes towards learning. There are no formal linkages between ICDS centers and primary schools that enable children to be prepared and which would encourage schools to the 'read for children.'

Skills and Competencies of Facilitators

For the effective and efficient implementation of ICDS programme, the role of the AWW is most crucial as they are the frontline functionaries who identifies beneficiaries and delivers the services. Educational Qualification of AWWs at the time entry into the service and training at the lateral stage to improve their competency level might be crucial factors to measure the skills of ECE facilitators. As far educational qualification is concerned, 12% of AWWs have attained education up-to primary standard, 20% have gone up-to middle standard, little less than half of the AWWs have completed education up-to 10th standard, and 18% of them have their educational qualification of higher secondary level or more. As far as training component within the ICDS programme is concerned, it is mandatory for all AWWs to go through one month job course training after joining 4-days are devoted for pre-school education training in the 30 days programs content of job training of AWWs. While AWWs viewed that the training had been useful in enhancing their skills for household, survey, immunization, health and nutrition education, record management, but it did not help them in improving pre-school education teaching skills.

Curriculum and Pedagogy

In the early childhood education stage, teaching-learning process and learning outcomes is equally important because what child learns has same significance with how child learns. ECCE is ought to be play-based, child centered and school based programme. Conversely, ECCE ought not to be syllabus-bound, teacher–centric and formal teaching programme. Pre-school education programme is integrated in ICDs with the objective to develop readiness of children for primary schooling. The ICDs guidelines of PSE has recognized that age group of 3-6 years is a school preparatory stage where emphasis should be on development of cognitive process along with motor and muscular development. The focus of pre-school education should be;

(i) To develop pre-number concepts;

(ii) Concept formation and language development though the activates like pre-conversation, storytelling, and vocabulary building. What is prescribed in pre-school curriculum called Arunima in Odisha is not practiced uniformly due to lack of orientation of the facilitator coupled with non-availability of appropriate materials and adequate space to conduct play based activities.

Due to lack of conceptual clarity about what is ECCE and what is not ECCE, AWWs are giving more stress to conventional method of teaching and formal learning such as reading, and writing.

Monitoring and Information Management

There is no proper system of monitoring and accountability mechanism is not present. Management Information System (MIS) is not developed properly or updated regularly to promote more research, evidence based planning and evaluation.

Key Findings

There is compelling evidence that pre-primary learning helps children to benefit from primary schooling, that it helps to prevent attrition in primary schools (especially where early grade primary education is well attuned to the early years and recognizes children's prior learning), and that it helps to promote high enrolment in primary school. All children should have access to pre-primary education to help them prepare for primary school. The pre-primary years are pre-requisite and the key to fulfilling the fundamental right to education. The 86th Constitutional Amendment Act 2002 changed the framework within which the Government of India fulfils its constitutional responsibilities for education.

Firstly, it inserted in Article 21-A into the Constitution of India to make school education for children aged 6-14 a statutory obligation on the state. Children aged 6-14 now have a fundamental right to school education. This right can be vindicated through the courts.

Further, the 2002 Act inserted Article-45 into the constitution, provides that the State shall endeavor to provide early childhood care and education for all children until they complete the age of six years and state authorities are empowered (but not compelled – Section-11 of RTE Act) to provide.

This aspirational provision does not appear to create a fundamental right to early education. It forms a Directive Principle of State Policy which state governments are expected take into account in framing local policies and programmes; but such principles are intended to be advisory rather than offering scope for interpretation and adjudication by the courts. While ECCE service in government sector is characterized by server gaps in provision and neglect of early childhood education, the services in private sector-which have expanded considerably are characterized by inequity and variable quality.

Parents in higher income groups are increasingly sending their pre-school children to private playgroups or to the nursery departments of private schools. This provision is entirely unregulated. In many cases, the provision takes the form of formal, school based learning intended to accelerate the child's performance in primary school. Thus ECCE in India is having reviewed the policy as well as examining the overall situation of early childhood education, the following suggestions are offered for bringing improvement in the system.

Secondly, strengthening basic infrastructure and support facilities holds the key to bring improvement in the quality of the service. Each centre should have own infrastructure with good physical environment and must have facility of safe drinking water, child friendly toilet, electricity.

Thirdly, what is needed for effective transaction of pre-school learning is well-motivated PSE Facilitator who has required knowledge, understanding, skills, and sensitivity to adopt a more professional approach towards education and development of children. A pre-school education training module has to be developed delineating activities to be conducted, process to be followed, and materials to be used by the facilitator for conducting pre-school education. Government is required to institutionalize pre-school education training for AWWs with the creation of nodal institute which may conduct training, and research on pre-school education.

Fourthly, a standardized PSE curriculum should be developed with the description of activity to be conducted, duration for each activity, methods to be followed to conduct each of the activities for age specific development of the child.

Fifthly, strong monitoring system should be put in place which must ensure multi-layer accountability in the governance of ICDS service. It needs to be develop with the information about the enrolment, attendance, outcomes of pre-school programme of ICDS in order to promote more research, evidence-based planning and evaluation.

Sixthly, considering the fact pre-school learning stage is a phase of transition for preparing the child for primary education, a system should be developed to ensure successful transition of the child from home to pre-school and form pre-school to primary school. Hence, birth of every child has to be registered and certified so that enrolment of the child for pre-school education at the right age may be ensured. Children completing pre-school education should be provided with pre-school leaving certificate in order to give this stage an added status and to ensure the entry of the child in primary class at the right age.

Last but not least, measures to improve the quality of early childhood education should include for early childhood education, development of teaching-learning materials, fund flow mechanisms. Reporting, accountability, and well delineated implementation modalities. There should be firm commitment on the part of the government to develop comprehensive legal framework so that early education provision should be governed, regulated and evaluated against common standards. The law must be contained with the provision for accessibility, quality, monitoring system, accountability mechanisms, funding pattern funds flow, modalities for community participation, and management information system.

References

1. Byrne, B. (1998). The foundation of literacy: the child's acquisition of the alphabetic principle. Hove, East Sussex, UK: Psychology Press.
2. Annual Activity Report 2012-13, Department of Women and Child Development, Govt. of Orissa.
3. Bredekamp, S. & Copple, C. (Eds.). (1997). Developmentally appropriate practice in early childhood programs: revised edition. Washington, D.C.: National Association for the Education of Young Children.
4. Census 2011, Govt. of India.
5. Economic Survey: 2012-13, Govt. of Orissa.
6. Gelman, R. & Baillargeon, R. (1998). A review of some Piagetian concepts. In P. Mussen, J. Flavell, & E. Markman (Eds.), Handbook of child psychology, Volume 3: Cognitive Development. New York: Wiley.
7. National Plan of Action for Children 2013, Govt. of India.
8. Seifert, K. (2001). Sociable thinking: Cognitive development in early childhood education. *Contemporary perspectives on early childhood education, pp. 15-40.* Greenwich, CT: Information Age Publishers.

9. State Plan of Action for Children 2009-12, Govt. of Orissa.
10. (http://www.waisman.wisc.edu/cls/).
11. http://www.orissadiary.com.

Notes

1. http://www.odisha.gov.in/portal
2. http://www.rchiips.org/nfhs/nfhs4.shtm, National Family health Survey: Health Survey
3. http://www.odisha.gov.in/portal
4. Website: www.clapindia.org. Email: ctk-committee@sancharnet.in

7

Early Childhood Care and Education: Contemporary Issues

Considering ECCE as the foundation of Education for All (EFA) agenda, UNESCO places highest priority for expanding and improving comprehensive early childhood care and education system. Many of the research findings reveals that good quality early childhood care and education programme have proven record in reducing dropout rates in primary schools, and improving learning achievements of children. The subject of ECCE is integrated with the Millennium Development Goals (MDG) and EFA Goals to which India is a signatory State. The Early Childhood Care and Education, is of invaluable significance for the holistic development of young children. The linkage of early childhood care and education with right to education has been a subject of considerable discussion across the world. International organization like UNICEF and UNESCO are stressing the importance of providing quality early childhood care and education to all children.

In India, ECCE received attention in National Policy for Education (1986) and POA (1992). It viewed ECCE is a crucial input in the strategy of human development as well as a feeder and support programme of Universal Elementary Education (UEE). However, with the enactment of 86th Constitutional Amendment Act, 2002, ECCE has found a place under the Artcle-45 of the Constitution of India which reads "State shall endeavor to provide early childhood care and education for all children, until they complete the age of six years". While education becomes a fundamental right for 6-14 years aged children, early childhood care and education is in Directives Principles of State Policy, which are non-justiciable.

The directive, under Article-45, "State shall endeavor to provide early childhood care and education." is only a direction and not a subject to judicial scrutiny if State fails to comply this constitutional obligation. The Early Childhood Care and Education (pre-school education) is made Section-11 of the Right of Children to Free and Compulsory Education Act, 2009. This law does not say anything about the service delivery mechanisms for ECCE.

Early Childhood Care and Education is considered as the all-important prerequisite to the realization of right to education (Article-21A), there is no legal framework on Article-45 in order to ensure early childhood care and education to all children of India. A vast numbers of children are deprived of getting quality early childhood care and education services. Children of rich and elite families have access to good quality private and special types of public schools for early childhood education, whereas children of poor and marginalized families are deprived of it or are integrated with the ICDS.

The Integrated Child Development Services (ICDS) is the largest programme in the country that offers a package services to 0-6 year aged children for their holistic development. ICDS is a programme of Government of India and it is being implemented in states and union territories with the financial assistance of central government. The ICDS is conceptually holistic, comprehensive, and integrated, but it is being poorly implemented at the ground level and it is also infatuated with delivering of poor quality service.

Constitutional Provision and the Scope of ECCE

A diligent effort should be made to assess the availability and opportunity for ECCE, and accessibility of children to early childhood care and education; and the kind of institutional facilities that have created by the state for delivering the ECCE service. Here the existing policies, schemes, and programmes are reviewed that are put in place for delivering the care and early childhood education to young children. The performance, service quality, infrastructure, basic facility, as well as human resource quality of ICDS Centers (Anganwadi Centers) at the ground have been assessed and evaluated through different means. The state of ECCE in the present policy framework is also illustrated. It also explores the legal dimension of Article-45 of the constitution in the absence of a statutory frame work to it. It elaborates the various dimensions of ECCE in reference to international child rights doctrines and world education declarations. Law, policies, and programes relating to ECCE/ECE/ECCD of selected countries are also presented in a comparative perspective with India. The conceptual framework of early childhood care and education has been built up with reference to philosophical views and cross-disciplinary theories on this subject. All in all, this is an analytical, exploratory, and comparative kind of study.

The notion of Early Childhood Care and Education (ECCE) is widely recognized as a process to develop school readiness habit of the child. The readiness of the child to school is interwoven with physical growth, psychological development, learning attitude, and cognitive development of the child. Early childhood is a period characterized with improvement of health, nutrition, and cognitive perception of the child. What can be more important for the State than to construct an ideal early childhood care and education programme, which should have balance linkage between the health, nutrition and early childhood education? ECCE should be recognized as the right and all children shall have opportunity to get quality early childhood care and education service. In view of these pre-conceived ideas, the following propositions are;

- ECCE is not recognized as a legal right in India even if there is constitutional direction to State to provide early childhood care and education to all children below 6 years age.

- The existing education policy frameworks in India have not integrated pre-primary education/early childhood education as the integral part of school education.
- Pre-school education is the most neglected component of the Integrated Child Development Service package.
- There is wide gap between ICDS policy prescription and implementation in practice.

However, the Constitution of India envisages that early childhood care and education (ECCE) should be made available to the children up to the age of 6 years. This Early childhood care and education (ECCE) was incorporated in the Constitution of India by 86th Constitutional amendment in the year 2002. Now this concept of Early Childhood Care and Education (ECCE) is in the Directive Principle of State Policy in Chapter-IV of the Constitution of India. The Constitution of India under its Article-45 inculcated the provision of Free and Compulsory education up to the age of 14. Then after it gets its Constitutional status under Article-21 (A) of the Constitution. It is incorporated in part III of Indian Constitution by the virtue of 86th Constitutional amendment.

Thus, there is need of to have a statutory back up to the provision of ECCE in Article-45. Early Childhood Care and Eeducation (ECCE) being a broader area of activity covers the physical, intellectual as well as psychological development of the child. Right of the Children for Free and Compulsory Education Act 2009 is unique one under which the Early Childhood care and Education (ECCE) is coming. Being a key concept for the successful transition of the child from Pre-primary to primary Education, ECCE is overlooked by the states. It defuses the perennial root cause for the failure of primary education in India as it has enough potential to prepare the children to attend primary education in the subsequent stage. In view of the significant role of ECCE in realizing the rights of the children, there is a need to provide a statutory back up to the provision of the ECCE in India so that it can be realized in a right based legal frame work.

ECCE aimed at the all round development of the children. By giving a statutory back up to the ECCE, it will be an enabling condition to secure access to primary education. The age 0-6 years of the child's life is considered as the most crucial one for the all round development of the child. It is therefore, the need of the hour to widen the scope of ECCE for the betterment of the child's physical, social as well as psychological development. Section-11 of the Right of the Children for Free and Compulsory Education Act, 2009 has strictly instructed the states to implement the pre-school provisions in their concerned State rules and implement them properly but it is all in vain.

The provision of the Early Childhood Care and Education as an important aspect and it was incorporated in the 86th constitutional amendment in the year 2002 and now it is coming under the 4th part of the Constitution i.e., the Directive Principle of State policy under Article-45 of Indian Constitution. Early Childhood Care and Education is an opportunity for the readiness of the children to attend the formal (Primary) education. Thus it focuses the importance of pre-primary education and care environment where health and nutrition are given adequate attention contains the root things of early childhood care and education.

The concept of ECCE (Early Childhood Care and Education) is understood as an integrated package of measures led by the Government of India for the fulfillment of the young children. These rights are recognized by the United Nations Convention on the Rights of the Child (UNCRC) which the Govt. of India ratified in 1992. The United Nations Convention on the Rights of the Child given maximum emphasis that early childhood care and education has its root in a rights based approach to the system of service for the young children especially the children from the age group of 3-6 years.

Thus the government should address the rights of the children in a holistic way so that their rights to education, health, nutrition, protection, affection etc. Early childhood care and education combines the elements from the field of child development, early childhood education, stimulation, health, nutrition, community development, parent education etc.

Perspectives and Perceptions about ECCE

The field realities of ECCE is to be reviewed in addition to direct interactions with teacher educators, heads of institutions, trainees and observations of classroom interactions, the study also sought perspectives of experts associated with the field of ECCE including teacher education in ECCE.

a) Field based perspectives and perceptions based on actual experiences of teacher educators, teacher trainees, alumni and school heads;

b) Perspectives and expectations of experts from the field of ECCE; and,

The views of experts are categorized as: (a) major concerns and (b) suggestions for improvement.

The Neglect of ECCE

There was almost a unanimous agreement amongst all experts that there is a collective lack of awareness regarding the importance of need for ECCE. They believed that we as a people, a community and as parents do not duly acknowledge the developmental needs of children in the early years and this lack of acknowledgement reflects in the non-serious attitude towards ECCE. This inevitably creates a vicious cycle wherein the indifference towards the needs of young children further translates into an inferior status of ECCE teachers, particularly in comparison to teachers of higher classes. This societal neglect also leads to a lack of quality training and trained professionals in ECCE and exclusion of ECCE in a Rights Perspective.

All experts expressed concern about the exclusion of children below 6 years in the Right to Education Act. In addition, concerns were expressed about the frequent violation of children's basic rights for safety, development and participation.

This concern is considered to be particularly significant because a large number of women in organized and unorganised sectors in rural and urban India work outside the home with the result that infants and young children receive inadequate care and stimulation. Experts also shared that while the ICDS programme is one of the largest in the world, the quality of care and support provided through Anganwadis and Balwadis is questionable. Is ECCE a Downward Extension of Formal Schools?

Another area of concern is the downward extension of the formal school curriculum into the pre-schools, wherein undue emphasis is placed on academic learning and formal education at the cost of appropriate development. Many pre-schools give marks as part of their evaluation practices and young children are required to score high marks in preschool in order to get admission in formal schools. According to some, "the children are put into a groove, almost a "prison like" rut of everyday grind to memorize the alphabet and numbers." Pre-schools, which were supposed to be an extension of the home and were to provide young minds with opportunities to develop their skills and critical thinking, have become a mere prelude to the formal school.

The experts attribute this to the uninformed expectations of parents, particularly the middle class, who perceive education as the means to a better life and believe that education has to start as early as possible. The practice of formal teaching with formal evaluation procedures in the early years robs children of their childhood. Some experts also articulated that such situations result in unhealthy development of children as adults, especially where natural experiences of play and sensitive social interaction are denied to young children. Responses of teacher educators and heads of teacher training institutions corroborate a gradual though still weak opening of new minds and perspectives in ECCE.

A few experts also articulated that there has been a relatively favorable change in the infrastructure of ECCE centers because of greater awareness about the need for 'attractive places' and child friendly infrastructure. This trend is being misused by pre-school chains that are commercially driven wherein young parents believe such centers to be good preschools'. Unfortunately, this further weakens the prevailing lack of understanding about appropriate practices in ECCE. There was almost a unanimous view among the experts that most teacher training programmes do not adequately prepare trainees to provide developmentally appropriate early education and to work competently in diverse socio-cultural settings. They believe that student teachers are prepared to follow only a "table-chair" approach for working at typical Perspectives and Perceptions Expectations from pre-schools that employ them are also limited due to their own narrow vision. Several experts expressed that many teacher education programmes do not expose teacher trainees to a variety of ECCE settings and do not adequately orient them to the contextual needs of such programmes.

Further, it was stressed that teacher education programmes do not adequately sensitise trainees to address the needs of children from diverse backgrounds. Developing a sense of respect for all communities and their customs, language, culture are very important and a common view was that this component is missing in most teacher education programmes. The experts felt that in order to address these gaps, changes need to be brought in at various levels, at the level of policy, at the level of the institutions and then further at the level of trainees and trained teachers.

Awareness about ECCE

Most experts emphasized the need for the development of policies in ECCE, both for the provision of facilities and their regulation. They felt that given the fact there is little awareness about the importance of ECCE, specific strategies need to be developed to create public awareness regarding developmentally appropriate early childhood education. Awareness needs to be developed amongst all stake holders simultaneously and collectively. Experts felt that efforts of this kind would ensure that children get the kind of childhood they deserve.

Changes in the Curriculum

Experts who had experience at the policy level felt that the curriculum in ECCE needs to be grounded strongly in education and psychology. They also felt that teacher training institutions needs to be strengthening the practical work component and provide greater exposure to different kinds of programmes for their trainees. Experts closely involved with training in ECCE articulated the need for a government policy in ECCE for regulation and approval of all kinds of ECCE centers and programmes in the country. Such regulations should also make it mandatory for appropriately trained professionals in ECCE to be employed in ECCE centers.

There was a clear division of perspectives about the need for a standardized curriculum for teacher education across the country. Half the experts felt that there should be a uniform curriculum for preparing teachers for Early Childhood Care and Education by the state and should be followed across the country to ensure homogeneity and standardization in the ECCE teacher education programmes. The other half, however, felt that the curriculum needs to be based on the needs and requirements of the particular state, region and community. They believe that the curriculum needs to be contextualized and adapted to the environment and potential employment sites of the trainees.

Monitoring of Programmes

A major area of concern expressed by almost all experts was the inadequate monitoring of various ECCE teacher education programmes. They strongly felt that certain standards need to be set and enforced. Institutions that follow prescribed standards should be given recognition and no private unrecognized institution should be allowed to operate. In order to follow such regulations, it is necessary that institutions be visited and monitored regularly. A few also suggested that institutions that do not follow norms should be shut down. It is felt that NCTE's role has been limited to being an affiliating body and its role in contributing to quality control appears to be weak.

Several experts mentioned that often individuals running teacher education programmes are unqualified and do not have adequate knowledge of ECCE or teacher education in ECCE. Experts also shared that there has been a surge in the number of recognized teacher training programmes in the past few years and many of these do not match the standards set by NCTE.

Some believe that lack of monitoring had led to the rise of many fraudulent institutions. Almost all experts indicated that there is a need to strengthen the monitoring mechanisms. Most experts were of the view that NCTE needs to set quality parameters for teacher education programmes and then enforce them strictly.

The 86th Constitutional Amendment Act-2002, by revising the provision of Article-45, made two important changes in the constitution. First is inculcation of Article-21 (A) in the fundamental rights chapter which pledge right to free and compulsory education of children aged 6-14 years. Second is inducting early childhood care and education for 0-6 years aged children in article 45 of directive principles chapter. Consequent upon the 86th amendment, Parliament of India enacted the Right of Children to Free and Compulsory Education Act, 2009 that understandably does not address the subject of early childhood care and education. It is a fact that early childhood care and education is the subject matter of ministry of women and child development and ICDS is the major programmes that address the issue. However, it is very often debated that access to ICDS service is neither universal nor legal. Whenever the ICDS performance is evaluated, a few pertinent issues and problems are repeatedly raised.

Facility Related Indicators

With the range of services being provided at AWCs, there are some pre-requisites in terms of infrastructure and basic amenities to be provided at the centre. Good physical environment and improved facilities at the centre could be the factor of inducement to catch up more and more beneficiaries to the anganwadis. But the fact that, a very little attention has been paid in the policy level for infrastructure development of anganwadis. As a result of casual approach of the government towards infrastructure development of ICDS programme at the service delivery level, AWCs do not have proper infrastructure to operate efficiently and effectively.

Quality Related Indicators

Quantitative expansion of ICDS centers does not ensure that service quality is improved. Mere increase in number of centers without quality assurance can be seen as a lop-sided improvement. Quality aspect of ICDS Programme it is in terms of two contexts, i.e. structural component of quality and process component of quality. Structural quality component of ICDS centre which includes physical infrastructure, basic and ancillary facilities such as drinking water, toilet, kitchen space, storage, and outdoor space etc. Some of the key findings of Process Quality Component such as competency of the facilitators, nature of curriculum and how it is used, availability of teaching-learning materials, teaching method followed, medium of teaching process.

For the effective and efficient implementation of ICDS programme, the role of the AWW is most crucial as they are the frontline functionaries who identify beneficiaries and deliver the services. Hence, they should receive intensive training about the context, content, curriculum, pedagogy, and methods of pre-school learning. As far as training component within the ICDS programme is concerned, it is mandatory for all AWWs to go through job course training after joining.

Management Related Indicators

ICDS is monitored at various levels. At the Central Level, the Ministry of Women and Child Development (MWCD) has overall responsibility of monitoring of ICDS. As far as pre-school education component of ICDS is concerned, State Governments are required to send consolidated report received from project level to Central ICDS Monitoring Unit which is placed under Ministry of Women and Child Development. At the Block Level, CDPO has responsibility for overall implementation of the scheme. Supervisors are placed at the cluster level with the responsibilities of supervising the AWC.

Involvement of community to support and supervise ICDS programme voluntarily is very minimal. Even though Mothers Committees have existence on record, the role of those committees is confined only for procurement, quality checking of food items for supplementary nutrition programme.

Physical and Motor Development: It refers to correct use hands and legs as well as control over the physical movement of the children. Physical and Motor Development Skills was assessed according to the ability of the child to do the following:

- Walk in straight line
- Throwing ball
- Catching ball
- Jumping

Language Development: It refers to child's ability to understand word, concept, sound he/she hear. Language development of the child was determined on the basis of following observations:

- Follow simple oral instructions such as to move, dance, and laugh.
- Recite a rhyme
- Name primary colours
- Identify sounds
- Identify body parts
- Identify animals
- Identify fruits and vegetables

Intellectual Development: It refers to child ability to differentiate, classify, and quantify the objects. Children should ask to do the following in order to measure the scale of their intellectual development:

- Name shapes
- Separate pieces by size
- Distinguish big or small
- Differentiate more or less
- Identify odd one

Preparatory Skills refers to child readiness to enter in primary schools. It was assessed on the basis of child's ability to do the following:

- Pronounce alphabets
- Trace alphabets from jumble
- Count numbers in forward and backward sequence
- Trace any number from jumble
- Holding pencil
- Copy alphabets
- Copy numbers
- Name days
- Name Month

Overview of ICDS

ICDS is a countrywide multi-dimensional programme of the Government of India that offers a comprehensive package of services to address the nutrition and health problems and to promote early childhood education. The objectives of the ICDS is to improve the nutritional and health status of children in the age group of 0-6 years:

- Lay the foundation for proper psychological, physical, and social development of the child.
- Reduce the incidence of mortality, morbidity, malnutrition, and school dropout.
- Enhance the capability of mother to look after the normal health and nutritional needs of the child through nutrition and health education.

ICDS is mandated to provide centre based pre-school education facility. Children of 3-6 years are offered with the benefit of non-formal pre-school education through the institution of Anganwadis. As per the ICDS guidelines, pre-school education has to be provided in a natural, joyful and stimulating environment with emphasis on necessary inputs for optimal growth and development of the child.

References

1. An Early Childhood Education Curriculum for the young children (3- 5 years), TN Forces, Chennai.
2. Ariel, S. (2002). Children's imaginative play. Westport, CT: Praeger.
3. Bissex, G. (1980). Gnys at work: A child learns to write and read. Cambridge, MA: Harvard University Press.
4. Bredekamp, S. & Copple, C. (eds.) (1997). Developmentally appropriate practice in early childhood programs: revised edition. Washington, D.C.: National Association for the Education of Young Children.
5. Early childhood spaces, by Alisan Clark, Bernad Van leer foundation, The Netherlands.
6. Gelman, R. & Baillargeon, R. (1998). A review of some Piagetian concepts. In P. Mussen, J. Flavell, & E. Markman (Eds.), Handbook of child psychology, Volume 3: Cognitive development. New York: Wiley.
7. National consultation on ECCD, issues and challenges for advocacy, Forces, New Delhi.
8. Seifert, K. (2001). Sociable thinking: Cognitive development in early childhood education. In O. Saracho & B. Spodek (eds.), Contemporary perspectives on early childhood education, pp. 15-40. Greenwich, CT: Information Age Publishers.
9. Anganwadi for all- Action for the rights of Anganwadi children fewer than six, by Devika Singh, Jean Dreze, Nandini Nayak, Vandana prasad, National Book Trust of India.
10. Early childhood spaces, by Alisan Clark, Bernad Van leer foundation, The Netherlands.

11. Gelman, R. & Baillargeon, R. (1998). A review of some Piagetian concepts. In P. Mussen, J. Flavell & E. Markman (Eds.), Handbook
12. National consultation on ECCD, issues and challenges for advocacy, Forces, New Delhi.
13. National consultation on ECCD, issues and challenges for advocacy, Forces, New Delhi.
14. National Plan of Action for Children (1992)

Index